David Maxwell

Bygone Scotland

Historical and social

David Maxwell

Bygone Scotland
Historical and social

ISBN/EAN: 9783743345232

Manufactured in Europe, USA, Canada, Australia, Japa

Cover: Foto ©ninafisch / pixelio.de

Manufactured and distributed by brebook publishing software (www.brebook.com)

David Maxwell

Bygone Scotland

BYGONE SCOTLAND:
HISTORICAL AND SOCIAL.

BY

DAVID MAXWELL, C.E.

"Stands Scotland where it did?"

EDINBURGH:
WILLIAM BRYCE, LOTHIAN STREET.
HULL:
WILLIAM ANDREWS & CO., THE HULL PRESS.
LONDON:
SIMPKIN, MARSHALL, HAMILTON, KENT & CO., LD.

1894.

Preface.

FOR a country of comparatively small extent, and with a large proportion of its soil in moor and mountain, histories of Scotland have been numerous and well-nigh exhaustive. The present work is not a chronicle of events in order and detail, but a series of pictures from the earlier history, expanding into fuller narratives of the more striking events in later times. And it includes portions of contemporaneous English history; for the history of Scotland can only be fully understood through that of its larger and more powerful neighbour.

The growth of a people out of semi-barbarism and tribal diversity, to civilization and national autonomy, is ever an interesting study. This growth in Scotland included many elements. The Roman occupation of Southern Britain banded together for defence and aggression the northern tribes. For centuries after the Roman evacuation the old British race held the south-

PREFACE.

western shires, up to the Clyde; the Anglo-Saxon kingdom of Northumbria extended to the Frith of Forth; there were Norse settlements on the eastern coast, in Orkney, and the Hebrides. Of the various races out of which the Scottish nation was formed, the Picts were the most numerous; but the Scots—a kindred race, wanderers from Ireland—were the more active and aggressive—came to assume the general government, and gave their name to the whole country north of the Solway and the Tweed.

It is interesting to trace how, in unsettled times, the burghs developed into little, distinct communities, largely self-governed. And the religious element in Scotland has been a powerful factor in shaping the character of the people and of the national institutions; the conflict of the Covenant was the epic in Scottish history. The rebellion of 1745, as the last specially Scottish incident in British history, is properly the closing chapter in *Bygone Scotland*.

D. M.

HULL LITERARY CLUB,
St. Andrew's Day, 1893.

Contents.

	PAGE
THE ROMAN CONQUEST OF BRITAIN	1
BRITAIN AS A ROMAN PROVINCE ...	12
THE ANGLO-SAXONS IN BRITAIN ...	18
THE RISE OF THE SCOTTISH NATION	26
THE DANISH INVASIONS OF BRITAIN ...	38
THE LAST TWO SAXON KINGS OF ENGLAND	48
HOW SCOTLAND BECAME A FREE NATION	63
SCOTLAND IN THE TWO HUNDRED YEARS AFTER BANNOCKBURN	73
THE OLDER SCOTTISH LITERATURE	80
THE REFORMATION IN ENGLAND AND SCOTLAND	85
THE RIVAL QUEENS, MARY AND ELIZABETH	102
OLD EDINBURGH	111
OFFENCES AND THEIR PUNISHMENT IN THE SIXTEENTH CENTURY	134
OLD ABERDEEN	152
WITCHCRAFT IN SCOTLAND ...	160
HOLY-WELLS IN SCOTLAND ...	166
SCOTTISH MARRIAGE CUSTOMS ...	172
SCOTLAND UNDER CHARLES THE FIRST ...	178
SCOTLAND UNDER CROMWELL	199
SCOTLAND UNDER CHARLES THE SECOND	211
SCOTLAND UNDER JAMES THE SECOND ...	236
THE REVOLUTION OF 1688 ...	252
THE MASSACRE OF GLENCOE	264
THE UNION OF SCOTLAND AND ENGLAND	270
THE JACOBITE RISINGS OF 1715 ...	279
THE REBELLION OF 1745	289

BYGONE SCOTLAND.

The Roman Conquest of Britain.

WE cannot tell—it is highly improbable that we ever shall know—from whence came the original inhabitants of the islands of Great Britain and Ireland. Men living on the sea-coasts of the great quadrant of continental land which fronts these islands, would, when the art of navigation got beyond the raft and canoe, venture to cross the narrow seas, and form insular settlements. It is indeed possible that, before that subsidence of the land of Western Europe which separated our islands from the mainland and from each other, was effected by the slow but ever-acting forces of geology, men were living on the banks of ancient rivers which are now represented by the Clyde, the Thames, and the Shannon.

The authentic history of Britain dates from the

Roman invasion; before this event all is myth and legend. Half a century before the commencement of our era, Julius Cæsar, whilst consolidating in strong and durable Roman fashion his conquest of Gaul, was informed by certain merchants of the country that on the other side of the narrow sea which bounded them on the north, there was a fertile land called Britain, or *the land of tin*. With his legions, in the trireme galleys of the period, Cæsar crossed the narrow sea, and, so far as he went, he conquered the land.

The inhabitants were in a rude condition of life; semi-barbarous perhaps, but certainly the peoples of Fingal and Ossian in the north, and of Caractacus and Boadicea in the south, had advanced far beyond simple savagery. Climatic and geographical influences had moulded into a robust, if a fierce and stubborn type, the common materials of humanity. The ancient Britons had, in their ideas of government, advanced beyond mere clan chieftainship. Their annals, in stone cairns and the songs of bards, commemorated bygone battles and deeds of warrior renown. They had a religion with its trained priesthood—it was not a religion of sweetness and light, but of ferocity and gloom, of human sacrifices, and mystical rites. Its temples and altars were clusters of huge stones, arranged in forest glades on some astronomical principles. The Druidic faith was one of the many offshoots of ignorant barbarism, in which the celestial orbs and the forces in terrestrial nature—lightning and tempest—life and fire— were deified. Its priesthood was a close order, holding in their mystical gripe the minds and lives of the people. It has been said that the ancient Britons were such firm believers in a future state, that they would even lend each other money, to be repaid in the spiritual world. Their language was a dialect of the Gaelic— the language spoken in more ancient times over the greater portion of Western Europe.

The Roman invasion under Julius was little more than a raid. He marched his legions as far inland as the Thames, and again retired to the coast; he left Britain without forming a Roman settlement, and for nearly a hundred years the island remained free, and did a considerable maritime trade with Gaul and Scandinavia. In A.D. 43, the fourth Roman emperor, Claudius, with a large army, invaded

Britain. The native tribes, although generally inimical to the Romans, had no concerted action amongst themselves, were often, indeed, at war with each other; and thus the disciplined soldiers of Rome had a comparatively easy task, although they had many fierce encounters with native bravery and hardihood. One British chief, Caractacus, held out the longest. He was the King of the Silurians, the dwellers in South Wales and its neighbourhood. For several years he withstood the masters of the world, but was ultimately defeated in battle, and he and his family were sent prisoners to Rome.

On the eastern coast, in what is now Suffolk and Norfolk, was a tribe called the Icenians. This tribe, under Boadicea, the widow of one of its kings, made, in the absence of the Roman governor, Suetonius, raids upon London, Colchester, and other Roman towns. When Suetonius returned, he defeated Boadicea in a battle near London. She killed herself rather than submit. Agricola succeeded Suetonius as governor, and he pushed the Roman Conquest northwards to a line between the Firths of Forth and Clyde. Beyond this line the Romans never made permanent conquests. Along this line

Agricola built a chain of forts as a defence of the Roman province against incursions from the northern tribes, and as a base of operations in attempting farther conquests. In a campaign in the year 84, he was opposed by a native force under a chief called Galgacus. A battle was fought amongst the Grampian Hills, near Blairgowrie, with a hardly-won victory to Agricola. It was such a victory as decided him to make the Tay the northern boundary of Roman occupation. But Roman fleets sailed round the northern shores,—planting the Imperial Standard on Orkney,—and returned, having proved that Britain was an island.

The northern portion of the island, beyond the line of forts, was then called Caledonia; border fighting was the rule, and the "barbarians from the hills" made frequent raids into the Romanized lowlands. Indeed, not only had the Romans to build a wall connecting the forts of Agricola, but also, as a second line of defence, one between the Tyne and the Solway Firth. The two walls prove the determination of the Romans to maintain their British conquests, and also at what a high rate they estimated the native resistance.

In 208, Serenus had to re-conquer the country

between the walls, restoring that of Agricola, and he carried the Roman eagles to the farthest points north which they ever reached. The remains of Roman roads through Strathearn to Perth, and thence through Forfar, the Mearns, and Aberdeen to the Moray Firth, belong to this period; and they represent attempts to subdue the whole island. Dion, the Roman historian, ascribes the failure of this attempt to the death of Serenus at York, in 241. He describes the Caledonians as painting on their skins the forms of animals; of being lightly armed; making rapid dashes in battle; of having no king, only their tribal chieftains. In 305, Constantius defeated the tribes between the walls; they are called in the Roman records, "Caledonians and other Picts;" the latter name being then used for the first time, and as being the more generic appellation. In 360, the Scots are named for the first time. They and the Picts made a descent upon the Roman province, and this is spoken of in terms which imply that they had previously passed the southern wall.

For about 366 years the Romans held sway in Britain; if we think of it, for as long a period as elapsed between Henry the Eighth's publishing his treatise in defence of the seven Romish sacraments, and the jubilee of Queen Victoria. The conquest of an inferior by a superior race is generally fraught with progressive issues to the conquered people. In the roads and architecture, the laws and the civic institutions of the country, the Romans left lasting memorials of their British rule. Towns rose and flourished; marshes were drained; the land was cultivated; low-lying coast lands were, by embankments, protected from the sea; trade advanced; Christianity and Roman literature were introduced.

As a constituent portion of the empire, Britain occupies a place in Roman history. A Roman commander in Britain, Albinus, had himself nominated emperor. He carried an army into Gaul, but was there beaten and slain in a battle with the rival emperor, Severus. Severus himself died at York, then called Eboracum; and, in 273, Constantine, since styled *The Great*, was born in that city, his mother, Helena, being British. Constantius, the father of Constantine, had a long struggle for the possession of Britain with Carausius, a Belgian-born Roman general, who, in 286, rebelled against the authority of the empire. The usurper formed a navy, with which he for eight years prevented Roman troops from landing on our shores, but he lost his life through treachery, and once more the imperial eagles floated over Britain. For a time Britain might be said to be the head-quarters of the empire. Residing principally at York, Constantius gave his commands to Gaul and Spain, to Italy itself, to Syria and Greece. It was in Britain that on the death of his father, in 306, Constantine was proclaimed emperor. He was the first Christian emperor, and all the emperors who succeeded him professed Christianity, except Julian, who, returning to the old gods, was called *The Apostate;* but Julian was really a wiser ruler and a better man than many of those who called themselves Christian. The new religion became the official faith of the empire. Not much is known with certainty of the early British church, but there are said to have been archbishops in the three chief cities, London, York, and Caerleon.

The grand old Latin language, containing in its literature the garnered up thoughts and attainments of centuries, spread its refining influences wherever the Roman camp was pitched. Latin was the official language in Roman Britain, and it would be known and probably spoken by the well-to-do Britons in the towns. But it never amalgamated with the old Celtic-Welsh of the common people. Celtic, although in many respects a well-constructed language, is not a pliant one—is not adapted for readily intermingling with other tongues. It has in its various dialects, which have through the succeeding centuries maintained their existence in Wales, in Ireland, and in the Highlands of Scotland, kept itself altogether apart from the English language; and it has given comparatively few of its words to the modern tongue.

In the third century the Roman empire was in its decline, and hastening to its fall. Constantine transferred the seat of government to Byzantium, and that city was thenceforth named from him, Constantinople; and then the Roman power was divided—there were eastern emperors and western emperors. In the Patriarch of the Greek Church residing in Constantinople and the Pope of the Catholic Church in Rome, we have that division perpetuated to this day.

The Romans had never been able to conquer more than small portions of the great country in Central Europe which lies north of the Danube and east of the Rhine, which we now call

Germany. One Teutonic chief called Arminius, afterwards styled *The Deliverer*, destroyed a whole Roman invading army. Towards the end of the fourth century the Teutonic nations began to press into the Roman empire, and one by one the provinces were wrested from it by these incursions. The Romans hired one tribe against another; but stage by stage the empire shrank in its dimensions, until it came to be within the frontiers of Italy; and still the barbarians pressed in.

On the 24th day of August, 410, the evening sun was gilding the roof of the venerable Capitol, and peace and serenity seemed to hover over the eternal city. But at midnight the Gothic trumpets sounded as the blasts of doom. No devoted Horatius now kept bridge and gate as in the brave days of old. Alaric, "the curse of God," stormed the city, to burn and slay and inflict all the horrors of assault; but sparing Christian churches, monks and nuns. It is said that forty thousand slaves in the city rose against their masters.

From the spreading of the Teutonic tribes, new nations were formed in Western Europe. The Franks pressed into Northern Gaul. Their name remains in Franconia, and in that portion of Gaul called France. In Italy, Spain, and Acquitaine, the Goths and other Teutonic peoples mingled with the Romans. From the Latin language, corrupted and mixed up with other tongues, arose the Italian, Spanish, Provençal, and French languages, all, from the name of Rome, called the *Romance* languages. The eastern empire still went on; in the sixth century it recovered for a time Italy and Africa. Its people called themselves Romans, but were not so much Roman as Greek. After a lengthened decline, its last fragments were destroyed by the Turks, who took Constantinople in 1453.

Britain as a Roman Province.

IT was fortunate for Britain that it came under the rule of Rome, not in the time of the Republic, when the conquered peoples were ruined by spoliation and enslavement; nor yet in the earlier years of the empire, a time of conflict and unsettlement, but after the death of the infamous Caligula, when Claudius had assumed the purple. At the beginning of the second century the Roman Empire was, under Trajan, at its culminating point of magnitude and power. Trajan was succeeded by Hadrian, whose governmental solicitude was shown in continuous journeying over his vast empire; and by the general construction of border fortification, of which the wall in Britain, linking the Tyne with the Solway Firth, is an example. Antoninus followed Hadrian, and of him it has been said: "With such diligence did he rule the subject peoples that he cared for every man of them, equally as for his own nation; all the provinces flourished under him." His reign was tranquil, and his fine personal qualities obtained for him the title of *Pius*. Of course for Britain it was the rough rule of military conquest; but it prevented tribal conflicts, secured order, and encouraged material development; corn was exported, the potter's wheel was at work, there was tin-mining in Cornwall, and lead-mining in Northumberland and Somerset; iron was smelted in the Forest of Dean.

But distance from the seat of government, as well as its murky skies, and wintry severity—no vines, no olive or orange trees in its fields—made Britain an undesirable land for Roman colonisation; it was held chiefly as a military outpost of the empire.

Whilst the more intimate Roman rule in South Britain gave there its civilizing institutions, its Latin tongue, its arts, laws, and literature, and in the fourth century Christianity, these results became less emphasized northwards—hardly reaching to the wall of Hadrian. The country between the walls remained in the possession of heathen semi-barbarians, scarcely more civilized or trained in the arts of civil government than were the Celtic tribes of the north. There were no Roman towns, and very few remains of Roman villas have been found, beyond York: remains of roads and camps, of altars and sepulchral monuments are found. To the south of York, Britain was a Roman settlement; north of York it was a military occupation.

In spite of its roads, its towns, and its mines, Britain was still, at the close of the Roman rule, a wild, half-reclaimed country; forest and wasteland, marsh and fen occupied the larger portion of its surface. The wolf was still a terror to the shepherd; beavers built their dams in the marshy streams of Holderness.

Unarmed, and without any military training, feeling themselves weak and helpless in the presence of the dominant race, the Britons of the province were yet sufficiently patriotic, to give negative help at least to the Pictish tribes who were ever making incursions into the district between the walls, and even at times penetrating into the heart of the province. One of these inroads in the reign of Valentinian all but tore Britain from the empire: an able general, Theodosius, found southern Britain itself in the hands of the invaders; but he succeeded in driving them back to their mountains, winning back for Rome the land as far as the wall of Agricola, and the district between the walls was constituted a fifth British province, named after the Emperor, Valentia.

And whilst the Pictish clans were thus making wild dashes over the walls, the sea-board of the province was harrassed by marauders from the sea. Irish pirates called Scots, or "wanderers," harried the western shores; whilst on the eastern and southern coast, from the Wash to the Isle of Wight, a stretch of coast which came to be called the Saxon Shore, Saxon war-keels were making sudden raids for plunder, and for kidnapping men, women, and children, to be sold into slavery. They also intercepted Roman galleys in the Channel, which were engaged in commerce, or on imperial business. In the year 364, a combined fleet of Saxon vessels for a time held the Channel.

And now the Romanized British towns began to shew their lack of faith in imperial protection, by strengthening themselves by walls. A special Roman commander was appointed, charged with the defence of the Saxon shore. The shore was dotted by strong forts, garrisoned by a legion of ten thousand men. The thick forests which lined the coast to the westward of Southampton water were considered sufficient guards against invasion in that quarter. As long as the Romans remained in Britain they were able to repel the attacks of their barbarous assailants. But when the fated hour came—when Rome in her death-struggle with the Teutonic hordes, whose gripe was at her throat in every one of her dominions in western Europe, and even in Italy itself, had to recall her troops from Britain—then the encircling foes closed in upon their prey.

In withdrawing, in 410, his troops from Britain, the Emperor Honorius, grandson of the general Theodosius we have mentioned, told the people in a letter to provide for their own government and defence. We may imagine how ill prepared, after ten generations of servitude, the Romanized Britons were for such an emergency. But they had fortified towns with their municipal institutions, and under the general sway of Rome they had lost their tribal distinctions, and become a more united people; and not in any one of the Romanized lands which became a prey to the barbarians did these encounter so prolonged and so energetic a resistance as in Britain. For some thirty years after the Roman evacuation of the province, it held out or maintained a fluctuating struggle with its enemies. The Scoto-Irish bucaneers were not only continuing their raids upon the western coast, but they planted settlements in Argyle to the north of Agricola's wall, and in Galloway—between the two walls. And the Picts were ever making incursions from the north. The policy was tried of hiring barbarian against barbarian. The Picts were the nearest and most persistent danger; and the marauders from over the North Sea,—Saxons, Angles, and Jutes, were, if not hired as mercenaries, permitted to hold a footing in the land, as a defence against Pictish invasion. About 450, three keels filled with Jutes, under two brothers, Hengist and Horsa, with a white horse as their cognisance, came by invitation from their own home—which is from them called Jutland—and landed on the Isle of Thanet on the eastern Kentish shore, making this their base for further conquests.

The Anglo-Saxons in Britain.

THE Teutonic nations from mid-Europe which, in their various tribes, conquered Italy, Spain, and Gaul, had had previous intercourse with the empire. Many had become Christians, and in their conquests they did not destroy. Their kings ruled the invaded lands, and their chiefs seized large portions of soil; but they adopted the provincial Latin tongues, and the general government was by Roman law. The clergy were mostly Romans, and they retained considerable power and estates. Thus the Goths, Visigoths, and Vandals did not become the peoples of the countries which they overran. The Teutonic element was absorbed into the national elements, largely resembling what afterwards took place in England, under the Norman Conquest.

But it was very different in Britain. Its Teutonic invaders—Jutes, Angles, and Saxons, had lived outside the influence of the empire; and indeed we know very little about them before they came to Britain. With the landing of Ella, in 477, Anglo-Saxon history may be said to begin. They were still heathens, and they knew nothing, and they cared nothing for the arts, the laws, or the language of Rome. Their object was not merely rule and authority over the Romanized Britons, but their destruction, and the entire occupation of the land. As they conquered, they killed the Britons or made them slaves, or drove them into Cornwall and Wales in the west, and into Caledonia in the north. They came over the North Sea in families, and thus propagated largely as an unmixed Anglo-Saxon race. But doubtless there were many more men than women in their bands, and there would be marriages with native women. Thus strains of British and Roman blood were left in the new occupants of what came to be England, and the lowlands of Scotland. The Anglo-Saxon tribes in Britain thus became a nation with its own language and laws, manners and customs. From the name of one tribe—the Angles—the southern and larger portion of the island came to be called *England*. *English* is the common language of Britain, and of its many off-shoots scattered over the habitable globe.

Kent—the nearest British land to the continent—bore the first brunt of Anglo-Saxon, as it had done of Roman, conquest. Then came Sussex (South Saxon). But the third settlement, that of Wessex (West Saxon), was a far larger one; taking in at least seven shires. It began in Hampshire, under Cedric, and his son Cynric—then styled Ealdermen—and gradually extended over all south-western Britain, and stretching northwards over Oxford and Buckingham shires. This was the era assigned to the legendary British King Arthur, fighting strongly for his native soil and his Christian faith, against the heathen invaders.

Another, the fourth Saxon kingdom, was that of Essex. And then there were three Anglian kingdoms—East Anglia, Northumbria and Mercia. East Anglia comprised Suffolk (South-folk), Norfolk (North-folk), and Lincolnshire. Northumbria included the country north of the Humber, as far as the Frith of Forth. That portion of Northumbria now known as Yorkshire was then called Deira, with York, then named Eboracum, its chief town; the portion north of the Tees was named Bernicia. The kingdom of Mercia, that is, of the *March*, had its western frontier to Wales, being thus the midlands of England.

And besides South Wales, including Cornwall, Devonshire, and the greater portion of Somersetshire, the old race still held a large district to the north of Wales, called Strathclyde, taking in Galloway and other districts in the south-east of what is now Scotland; together with Cumberland, Westmoreland, and Lancashire, down to the river Dee, and the city of Chester; they, even to the end of the sixth century, held portions of west Yorkshire, including Leeds.

The Anglo-Saxon occupation having thus at the close of the sixth century resolved itself into seven independent governments, is hence called the Heptarchy. But the division was not a lasting one. The conquerors, although a kindred race—with one understood language—and one old Scandinavian faith, were far from being a homogeneous people. They had tribal proclivities, and were generally at war with each other— "battles of kites and crows," Milton wrote. At times one king was powerful, or of such personal superiority to his neighbours, that he assumed a suzerainty over them, and was called a *Bretwalda*. But the Anglo-Saxon kings were not autocrats;

they had to consult their Witans—their council of "witty or wise ones." And there was in society the elements of what came to be feudalism. The King had his Thanes, or Earls; and these had their *churls*, who, holding lands under their lords, were expected to follow him in the wars. And there was slavery; men were made slaves who committed crimes, or were taken prisoners in war.

The seventh century witnessed in Anglo-Saxon Britain the conversion from the old Norse belief in Odin, Thor, and Fries to the Christian faith. Not from their British slaves, nor from the independent British of Wales and Strathclyde, did the new faith reach them. In 597, Pope Gregory sent Augustine and a number of other monks to preach Christianity in England. The most powerful ruler in Britain at this time was the Kentish king, Ethelbert; he was Bretwalda, exercising some authority over all the kings south of the Humber; and he had married a Frankish wife who was a Christian. The King received the missionaries kindly; and they preached to him and his chief men through interpreters. In a short time the King and a number of his people were baptized. Augustine made Canterbury his headquarters, and it has ever since been the chief See of the Anglican Church.

In 635, Oswald, King of Northumbria, routed a British Strathclyde army, largely shattering this kingdom of the older race; it was as much as the Welsh could do to hold the country west of the Severn.

In this seventh century, Devon and the whole of Somersetshire became English. Oswald was now Bretwalda, and Northumbria, in the struggles for supremacy of the Saxon kingdoms, was for a generation the foremost power. It also became Christian, but more from the labours of Scottish missionaries from Iona, than from the successors of Augustine.

In early life, Oswald, during an exile amongst the Scots, had visited Iona, and there became acquainted with Christianity. On his return he founded a monastery on Lindisfarne, thence called Holy Isle; a Scottish Bishop, Aidan, he placed at its head; a succeeding Bishop, Cuthbert, was the most famous of the saints of Northern England. And the Christianity which came to Scotland from Ireland through Columba, himself a Dalriadan Scot, differed in many ways from that which had come from Rome.

Not only did they differ in ritual, in dates of festivals, and in the shape of the monkish tonsure, but in what was of more political importance—ecclesiastical discipline and organization. The Church of Augustine implied dioceses, bishops in gradation of rank and authority, culminating in the Bishop of Rome as the head of the Church. The Church of Columba was a network of monasteries, a missionary church full of the zeal of conversion, but wanting in the power of organization. And thus there was conflict between the two churches, and this conflict was an important factor in the political history of the times. Ultimately the policy of Rome prevailed. The country was divided into dioceses, the loose system of the mission-station sending out priests to preach and baptize as their enthusiasm led them, gave place to the parish system with its regular incumbency, and settled order.

In the beginning of the ninth century the strife for headship over the others, which had been long waged by the kings of the stronger kingdoms, was terminated by the Northumbrian Thanes owning Egbert, King of Wessex, as their over-lord. Egbert defeated the Britons in

Cornwall, brought Mercia under his rule, and united all the territories south of the Tweed. The Kings of Wessex were henceforth, so far as Anglo-Saxon rivals were concerned, Kings of England.

The Rise of the Scottish Nation.

IN the second century, Ptolemy, the Egyptian astronomer, composed the first geography of the world, illustrated by maps. He would probably get his information about Britain—which was still called Albion—from Roman officers. What is now England, is shown with fair accuracy; but north of the Wear and the Solway it is difficult to identify names, or even the prominent features of the country; and the configuration of the land stretches east and west, instead of north and south.

The Celts were not indigenous to Britain. It is hardly possible to trace in any—in the very earliest peoples, of whom history or archæology can speak—the first occupants of any one spot on the earth. Science is ever pushing back, and still farther back, the era of man's first appearance as fully developed man upon the globe. And in his families, his tribes, and his nations, man has ever been a migrant. Impelled by the necessities of life, or by his love of adventure or of conquest, he has changed his hunting and grazing grounds, made tracks through forests, sought out passes between mountains; and the great, all-encompassing sea has ever been a fascination; the sound of its waves a siren-song inciting him to make them a pathway to new lands beyond his horizon. Before the Celtic Britons dwelt in this island in the northern seas, which they have helped to a great name, there were tribes here who had not yet learned the uses of the metals, whose spear-heads and arrow-tips were flints, their axes and hammers of stone. But the Celts were of that great Aryan race, tribes of which, spreading westwards over Europe, had carried with them so much of the older civilization of Persia, that they never degenerated into savagedom. The Britons were probably in pre-Roman times the only distinctive people upon the island.

How came the Celts to Britain? Probably colonies from Old Gaul first took possession of the portions of Britain nearer to their own country; and gradually spreading northwards, came in time to be scattered over what is now England and Wales, and the Lowlands of Scotland. Ireland being in sight of Britain from both Wigton and Cantyre, adventurers would cross the North Channel, and become the founders of the Irish nation.

The Picts—a Latin name for the first northern tribes whom the Romans distinguished from the Britons—called themselves *Cruithne*. Their earliest settlements in and near Britain appear to have been in the Orkneys, the north-east of Ireland, and the north of Scotland. They must then have made considerable advancement in the art of navigation. At the time of the Roman invasion, the southern Britons called the dwellers in the northern part of the island *Cavill daoin*, or "people of the woods,"—and thus the Romans named the district Caledonia. It has been surmised that the Picts of ancient Caledonia were a colony of Celtic-Germans; for such offshoots from the parent race occupied portions of central Europe. There was the same element of Druidism; but the Druids in Caledonia declined in influence and authority at an earlier date than did their brethren in Wales and South Britain. The bards took their place in preserving and handing down—orally and in verse—the traditions of their tribes—the heroism and virtues, the loves and adventures, of their ancestors. It may be noted that whilst in this early poetry the spirits of the dead are frequently introduced, and the powers of nature—sun, moon, and stars, the wind, the thunder, and the sea—are personified, there is no mythology,—no deities are called in to aid the heroes in battling with their foes.

By the end of the Roman occupation, the Caledonian Picts had spread down east and central Scotland as far as Fife. And there are Pictish traces in Galloway on the west coast; probably a migration from Ireland. After the Romans left, the Picts, in their southern raids, so often crossed and made use of Hadrian's wall, that the Romanized-Britons came to call it the Pictish wall. Their language was a dialect of Celtic, afterwards coalescing with, or being absorbed in, the Gaelic of the Scots, and which came to be the common tongue in the Highlands and western isles; but it was never a spoken tongue in the Scottish Lowlands.

The Scots are first found historically in Ireland; and they were there in such numbers and influence, that one of the names of Ireland from the sixth to the twelfth century was Scotia. Irish traditions represent the Scotti as "Milesians from Spain;" Milesia was said to be the name of the leader of the colonizing expedition. But their Celtic name of Gael sounds akin to Gaul. Their history in Ireland forms an important factor in the annals of that country. Those of the Irish people who considered themselves the descendants of the earlier colonists of the island never came heartily to recognise as fellow-countrymen,—although these had been for many generations natives of the land,—the descendants of those who settled at a later date. On the other hand—and similarly keeping up old race hatreds and lines of demarcation—the descendants of the later settlers looked upon themselves as a superior race, and never heartily called themselves Irishmen. This restricted and mock patriotism, aggravated by religious differences, has almost made of the Irish people two nations.

The Scotti must have made considerable settlements in North Britain in the second or third century, or they would not have been in a position to join the Picts in attacks upon the Roman province in the fourth century. When we come to enquire who were the peoples associated with the Christian missionary Columba in the latter half of the sixth century, we find that the districts bordering the east coast down to the Firth of Forth, and the central Highlands, with the chief fort at Inverness, were peopled by Picts; and that Scots were in Argyle and the Isles as far north as Iona. Their settlement around the shores of Loch Linnhe—the arm of the sea at the entrance to which Oban now stands—became in time a little kingdom called Dalriada, which gradually shook off the overlordship of the Scotic kings in Ireland, and maintained itself against the Picts on its northern and eastern borders. A British king ruled in Strathclyde, which included the south-west of Scotland up to the Clyde; and, bordering on Strathclyde, Anglo-Saxon Northumbria included the east of Scotland up to the Forth. Up to this time the Celts in North Britain had left no written history behind them; indicating that they were less civilized than their Welsh and Irish kin. It is in the annals of Beda and other Anglo-Saxon writers that we find anything like trustworthy history after the departure of the Romans. The Romanized Britons got Christianity from their rulers, but subjection to the Bishop of Rome was not transmitted with the faith. The British bishops, at their meeting under St. Augustine's oak, declined to submit to the missionary from Rome.

It is usually said that Scotland gave Patrick to Ireland. It was a strange kind of *giving*. Shortly after the Roman exodus, amongst a number of Britons taken captive by a Scotti-Irish raid on the banks of the Clyde, was a young lad of sixteen, who was sent as a slave to tend sheep and cattle in Antrim. The people round him were idolators; but in the solitude of the pastures he nursed the Christian faith of his childhood, and burned with the zeal of a young apostle for the conversion of the land. For ten years he remained in captivity, then he made his escape, and after many wanderings, reached his old home. Ordained a priest, and in time a bishop, he set manfully to realize in Ireland the dream of his youth, and he had abundant success. He founded churches, seminaries, and monasteries; the new faith spread like wildfire over the land.

And a century later, in 563, thirty-three years before the Roman mission of Augustine, Ireland sent over Columba to Britain. He, with twelve companion monks, founded on the little isle of Iona a monastery, which became the centre of Christianity in North Britain. The Scotti who had settled in the neighbouring islands, and on the nearest mainland, were already Christians.

But Columba visited and converted the Pictish King Bruda, and founded a number of churches and monasteries. Than Iona there is no spot of greater historical interest in the United Kingdom; but none of the ecclesiastical ruins found there date from Columba. The first buildings were of wood, but the original foundations in Skye and Tiree were his work. Columba was also a warrior, taking a strong part in several campaigns in Ireland, as a liegeman of the Scotic King. The disciples of Columba were called Culdees, meaning, from their monastic life, "sequestered persons." The Pictish bard Ossian is said, when blind and in old age, to have met and conversed with one of these Culdees. After ten years of prosperous rule in Iona, Columba contributed to start into greater unity and more vigorous life the Scotic settlement of Dalriada. He consecrated a young chieftain, Aedhan, as king; and Aedhan drove the Bernicians from the debatable land south of the head-waters of the Forth, and formed a league of Scots and Strathclyde Britons against Northumbria itself. But the league was, in 603, defeated by the Northumbrian King Ethelfrith in a great battle. The Scots were thrown back into their Highland fastnesses, and Beda says, writing a hundred years later, "From that day to this no Scot King has dared to come into battle with the English folk." Ethelfrith, by another victory over the Welsh at Chester, in 611, and further successes up to Carlisle, divided by a great gap the Kingdom of Strathclyde from North Wales, and it became tributary to Northumbria. On the decline of Northumbria, in the eighth century, Strathclyde re-asserted its independence; and, in a restricted sense, its extent, more nearly answered to its name, "The Valley of the Clyde." With Galloway, it continued under its own rulers, until, in the tenth century, it was connected with the Kingdom of Scone by the election to its throne—if it could afford a throne—of Donald, brother of Constantine II., King of Scots.

The Picts whom Columba converted appear to have been then consolidated under one monarch, Brude; his rule was from Inverness to Iona on the west; on the north to the Orkneys—probably including Aberdeen; its southern boundary is undefined. Of succeeding kings to Brude, there is a list of names; but little is known of the men themselves until, in 731, we come to Angus Mac-

Fergus. In reprisal for the capture of his son by Selvach, King of the Dalriad Scots, he attacked Argyle, and reduced the whole western highlands. The Strathclyde Britons were assailed by a brother of Angus, in 756, and their chief town, Alclyde,. destroyed. In the beginning of the ninth century, the seat of the Pictish government appears to have migrated from Inverness into Perthshire,—Scone becoming its political capital.

The history of the Dalriadan Scots, although interwoven with that of the Picts, and meeting at many points with the histories of the Britons of Strathclyde, and the Angles of Northumbria, is yet misty and legendary. True, there is a list of kings, and their stalwart portraits hang in the great hall of Holyrood; so extensive is this list, that if they had reigned for anything like an average period, it would carry the history back to about three hundred years B.C.

We find something like a trustworthy beginning in Fergus, the son of Earac, in 503. From this date for upwards of two hundred years, down to Selvach, who was conquered by the Pictish King Angus Mac-Fergus, there is from the *Irish Annals*, and the *Church*

History of Beda, a reasonable certainty. After this there is another century of hazy legend. If, as seems probable, Dalriada continued through the latter seventy years of the eighth, and the first half of the ninth century, under Pictish rule, it is not easy to see how, in the middle of the ninth century, Kenneth Mac-Alpine, called in the *Irish Annals* a king of the Picts, founded, as there is no doubt he did, a line of Scottish monarchs on the throne of Scone. One hypothesis is, that Kenneth was the son of a Pictish king by a Scottish mother, and by the Pictish law, the mother's nationality determined that of the children. Whatever the circumstances of the case, the accession of Kenneth Mac-Alpine represents an era in Scottish history. There was thenceforth such a complete union of Scots and Picts, that as separate races they lost all distinctiveness. But it certainly appears that, both by numerical superiority and historical prestige, the country should have been Pictland, rather than Scotland.

The kingdom of Kenneth included central Scotland from sea to sea, Argyle and the Isles, Perthshire, Fife, Angus, and the Mearns. Lothian was still Northumbrian. The Vale of the Clyde,

Ayr, Dumfries, and Galloway, were under a British king at Dumbarton. There were several independent chieftains in Moray and Mar; and Orkney and the northern and north-western fringes of the country, were dominated by Norsemen.

The Danish Invasions of Britain.

IN the first quarter of the ninth century, invaders from lands farther north than Jutland—hence called Norsemen—played broadly the same parts in Britain as the Angles and Saxons had played three hundred years previously. These Norsemen, in their war galleys, prowled over the Northern Seas, plundering the coasts, and making first incursions and then settlements in Muscovy, Britain, and Gaul. They discovered and colonised Iceland. Many centuries before Columbus, they had sailed along the coast of North America, and even attempted settlements thereon. On the northern coast of France, Normandy, under its powerful dukes, had become almost an independent state.

In their English invasions they are commonly called Danes, but in their own homes they formed three kingdoms, Norway, Sweden, and Denmark. Probably the invaders of England were mainly Danes. They were still "heathens," *i.e.*, of the old Scandinavian faith; and they held the Christian faith in supreme detestation. They were daring, fierce, and cruel; but still people of a kindred race, speaking dialects of the same Teutonic tongue; and when they settled in the land and became Christians, their language and manners differed so little from those of the Anglo-Saxons, that they did not remain a separate nation, as the Anglo-Saxons did from the British. It was more as if another Teuton tribe had come over and become joint occupants of the land. But, to begin with, they came as plunderers, taking their booty home. They ravaged Berkshire, Hampshire, and Surrey, destroying churches and monasteries. They invaded and took possession of East Anglia. They penetrated into Mercia; at Peterborough they burned the minster, slaying the abbot and his monks. They made extensive settlements in Yorkshire and Lincolnshire.

In 876, the Danes invaded Wessex, of which Alfred—one of the grandest names in old English history—was then King. Alfred had to fight the invaders both on sea and land. In and about Exeter there were several engagements, resulting in the Danes agreeing to leave Alfred's territories. Two years later they broke truce, made a sudden incursion to Chippenham, and became for a time masters of the west country. This is the time assigned to the neatherd-cottage negligence of Alfred, in allowing the cakes to burn in baking, whilst sheltering amongst the wood and morasses of Somersetshire. After a time he organised a sufficient army to meet, fight with, and beat the Danes—they gave him oaths and hostages against further disturbance, and their King Guthrum—thence called Athelstan—with thirty of his chief followers were baptized. But the Danes now held East Anglia, Northumbria, and large portions of Essex and Mercia,—indeed more than one-half of what is now England. Alfred being in peace during the latter years of his reign, devoted himself to works of governmental utility, he made a digest of the laws, and saw that justice was impartially administered; and he was the father of the English navy. His mind was cultured with the best learning of the times, and he made Anglo-Saxon translations of the Psalms, of Æsop's Fables, and of Bede's Church History.

In the first year of the tenth century, Alfred's son, Edward (styled the Elder, so as not to confuse him with later Edwards), began a reign of

THE DANISH INVASIONS OF BRITAIN. 41

twenty-five years. He was a strong king; through all his reign he had conflicts with the Danes, who had settled in the north and east of England; always beating them, and then having to quell fresh insurrections. And he made himself Over-King of the Scots and Welsh; so he was the first Anglo-Saxon king who became lord of nearly all Britain. Wessex, Kent, and Sussex he had inherited, Wales, Strathclyde, and Scotland acknowledged him as Suzerain. His son, Athelstan, succeeded him in 925; and the King of England now held such a high place among the rulers of Western Europe, that several of his sisters married foreign kings and princes. In 937 a great battle was fought in the North, when a combination of Scots under Constantine, and Danes and Irish under Anlaf, were defeated with much slaughter by Athelstan. It is called by the old chroniclers the Battle of Brunanburg, but the locality is uncertain. Constantine and Anlaf escaped; but Constantine's son was killed, as, says the old chronicler, were "five Danish Kings and seven Jarls."

Athelstan died in 941. Two of his brothers, and one brother's son occupied the throne successively during the next eighteen years.

Then, in 959, Edgar, a grandson of Alfred, then only sixteen years of age, was by the Witan made King. He was called *The Peaceable;* during his reign of sixteen years, no foe, foreign or domestic, vexed the land. Northumbria, extending as far north as the Forth, with Edwinsburh its border fortress—garrisoned by Danes and Anglo-Saxons—having long been a trouble to the Kings of Wessex, Edgar divided the earldom. He made Oswulf Earl of the country beyond the Tees—including the present county of Northumberland; and Osla, Earl of Deira, where the Danes had ruled, with York for his chief town; but the Danes were allowed to live peaceably under their own laws. And Edgar granted Lothian, containing the counties of Linlithgow, Edinburgh, and Haddington, to Kenneth, King of Scots, to be held under himself. And thus Lothian was ever after held by the Scottish Kings, and its English speech became the official language of Scotland. With Strathclyde, west of the Solway, under a Scottish prince, the map of the Kingdom of Scotland was now broadly traced out.

Edgar commuted the annual Welsh tribute to 300 wolves' heads. He appointed standard weights and measures, maintained an efficient fleet, and was altogether a fine example of a man who—although of small stature and mean presence—by vigour of mind and will, ruled ably and well in rude times. He was really *Basileus*, —lord-paramount of all Britain. After his coronation at Bath, which was not before he had reigned thirteen years—he sailed with his fleet round the western coasts. Coming to Chester, it is related that eight Kings, viz.: Kenneth of Scotland, Malcolm of Cumberland, Maccus of the Western Isles, and five Welsh princes did homage to him. They are said to have rowed him in a boat on the Dee—he steering—from the palace of Chester to the minster of St. John, where there was solemn service; and then they returned in like manner.

But these halcyon days for England of peace and settled government ended with Edgar. He died in 975, leaving two sons—Edward by a first wife—Ethelred by a second. Edward succeeded, but reigned only four years, being assassinated at the instigation of his step-mother, who desired the crown for her son. Edward was in consequence styled *The Martyr*. Ethelred was named *The Unready*. He was weak, cowardly, and thoroughly bad; his long reign of thirty-eight years, was one duration of wretchedness and confusion. He had hardly begun to reign when the foreign Danes began to be troublesome, and this time it was a farther stage of invasion: they meant not plunder or partial settlement, but conquest!

In the first quarter of this tenth century, the Northmen had taken possession of a large district on the north of France. Their leader, Rolf Ganger, became a Christian—or at least was baptized as such,—married the daughter of Charles the Simple, King of the West Franks, and was, as Duke of Normandy, confirmed in his possessions—a territory on either side of the Seine, with Rouen for its capital. And after this, the Danes and other Northmen, in their expeditions against England, had assistance from their kinsfolk in Normandy.

Ethelred tried first to bribe the Danes to leave him in peace; and for the money for this purpose he levied the first direct tax imposed upon the English nation. It was called Dane-gild, and amounted to twelve pence on each hide of land, excepting lands held by the clergy. But the idea was a vain one, for whilst the tax was vexatious, the pirate-ships still swarmed along the English shores. In 1001, the Danes, under King Sweyn, attacked Exeter, but were repulsed by the citizens. Then—beating an English army—they ravaged Devon, Dorset, Hants., and the Isle of Wight; loading their ships with the spoils. Next year Ethelred gave them money; but finding this of no use, he devised the mad and wicked scheme of ordering a general massacre of the Danes residing in England. On St. Bryce's Day this massacre, to a large extent, took place; it included aged persons, women, and children. Gunhild, a sister of Sweyn's, was one of the victims. Burning for revenge, Sweyn again invaded England. Exeter he now took and plundered, and again marched eastwards through the southern shires. He was generally successful, for there was treason and incompetency amongst the English leaders; and the unpopularity of Ethelred was a down-drag on the English cause. Year after year, Sweyn's fleets appeared on the fated coasts, and the Danes marched farther and farther inwards. Through East Anglia they went into the heart of England, burning Oxford and Northampton.

In August, 1013, Sweyn sailed up the Humber

and Trent to Gainsborough. Here he had submission made to him of the Earl of Northumbria, and of the towns of Leicester, Lincoln, Nottingham, Stamford, and Derby. He then marched to Bath, where the western Thanes submitted to him, and then London submitted. Ethelred and his queen fled to Normandy, Emma, the Queen, being the Duke's sister, and Danish Sweyn was virtually King of England. But he did not long enjoy his conquest; early in 1014 he died at Gainsborough.

Canute, the son of Sweyn, was a man of strong will, and he had already achieved warrior renown: but he had a severe struggle before he secured his father's conquests. First, after Sweyn's death, the Witan, after extorting promises that he would now govern rightly, recalled King Ethelred. Receiving better support, and his son Edmund, named Ironside, being an able commander, he defeated Canute, who had to take to his ships. Then Ethelred died, and Canute returned. There was much fighting,—London being twice unsuccessfully assaulted by the Danes,—and then the rival princes, Edmund and Canute, had a conference on a little island in the Severn. They agreed to a division of the kingdom,—the Saxon district to be south,—and the Danish district to be north of the Thames. A few weeks after the treaty, Edmund died, and although he left a young son Edward, Canute became sole monarch. For twenty-four years,—1017 to 1041, —England was under Danish rule. Canute married Emma, the widow of King Ethelred, and he further tried to win over his English subjects by sending home all Danish soldiers, except a bodyguard of 3000 men. Besides England, he ruled over the three Scandinavian kingdoms in the north, and is said to have exacted homage from Malcolm, King of Scotland, and his two under-kings. He was the first Danish King who professed Christianity. He introduced the faith into Denmark, and himself made a pilgrimage to Rome. He reigned nineteen years, dying in 1036.

After Canute's death, the Witan divided England into two portions. The counties north of the Thames, including London, were assigned to Harold, a son of Canute by his first wife; and the district south of the river to Hardicanute, his son by Emma. Harold died in 1039, and Hardicanute became sole King. He died two years later, and before he was buried, his half-brother Edward, the son of Ethelred and Emma, and thus a descendant of Alfred, was chosen King.

The Last Two Saxon Kings of England.

A NOTABLE personage, Earl Godwin, was the chief influence in this reversion to the old race. Who was Earl Godwin? In 1020, Canute, having come to trust his English subjects, and wishing to mix the two nations in the administration of affairs, created Godwin Earl of the West Saxons. He was an able administrator, an eloquent speaker, of high courage, and these qualities generally exerted for the freedom and independence of his country; and he came to have the greatest personal influence of any man in England. Little is known with certainty of his birth, but he married Gytha, the sister of Ulf, a Danish Earl, who had married a sister of Canute, and whose son, Sweyne, became after the death of Hardicanute, King of Denmark. Godwin had several children, all of whom occupy conspicuous places in the history of this eleventh century; the second son, Harold, being the last of the Saxon Kings of England.

Earl Godwin became the King's chief minister,

and the King married his daughter Edith. The King lived an ascetical, monkish life, and they had no children. Edward had been born in England, but on the deposition of his father Ethelred, his mother Emma took him to the court of her brother Robert, Duke of Normandy; and he had lived there through the reigns of Canute and Harold, coming back to England with Hardicanute. He was thus thoroughly Norman-French in his speech and his manners,—very fond of his young cousin, Duke William, and he now gathered French people about him, and promoted them to office and estate. The French language and fashions prevailed at Edward's court; and in this language lawyers began to write deeds, and the clergy to preach sermons. These foreign modes, so different from the English, gave great displeasure to the old nobles; and Earl Godwin—although three of his sons had been advanced to earldoms—rebelled against the King's authority. After some fighting, the Earl's army deserted him at Dover, and he had to seek refuge in Flanders. His daughter, the queen, was deprived of her lands, and sent to a nunnery of which the King's sister was abbess.

At the outbreak of the revolt, Edward asked

aid from William; the aid was not required, but William, then twenty-three years of age, came, with a retinue of knights to his cousin's court. They were hospitably entertained, and it is said that the King promised to bequeath his crown to William.

Things did not go on well during Godwin's absence, so when, in 1052, he and his sons appeared with a fleet in the Channel, there was an under-current of mutiny in the King's ships under their French commanders. "Should Englishmen fight with and slay Englishmen, that outlandish folks might profit thereby?" So the King had to take Godwin back into his honours and estates: but he died next year, leaving to Harold his titles, and his place as foremost man in England.

And now the dangers of a disputed succession loomed over England. The Witan advised Edward to send for Edward, the son of Edmund Ironside, then an exile in Hungary. Edward came with his family—a son Edgar, and three daughters: but he died shortly after his arrival. About this time Harold was shipwrecked on the Norman coast; William kept him prisoner for some time, and under circumstances of fraud and

LAST SAXON KINGS OF ENGLAND. 51

chicanery, an oath was extorted from him to favour William's pretensions to the English throne. Edward died on 5th January, 1046, at the age of 65. He was buried next day in Westminster Abbey, which he had built. There, in the centre of the magnificent pile, is his shrine, for, about a century after his death, he was canonised, and awarded the title of *Confessor*.

And now, who was to be chosen King of England? For a choice had to be made. Edgar the Atheling was quite young, and was hardly English—having been born and brought up in a foreign land; so, in these unsettled times, he was not thought of. The Witan were obliged to do what had never previously been done in English history, and has never been done since (except partially, in the case of calling William of Orange to reign jointly with his wife Mary),—to choose a King not of the blood royal.

But it was not a difficult choice. Amongst the nobles of England, one man, Harold, stood foremost, both in strength of position and in personal qualifications. He had now for years been the chief administrator—a born ruler of men —energetic yet prudent—valiant without ferocity ; and he had been the later recommendation of

Edward as his successor. So, on the very day of Edward's burial, Harold was crowned in the same Abbey, King of England.

Harold's troubles began almost from the day of his coronation. William sent demands for the crown; Edward had promised it to him, the King's nearest of kin, and Harold had sworn over concealed relics, to help him to it. It was replied that the crown was not disposable by Edward; all he could do was to recommend a successor to the Witan; and this he had done in favour of Harold: Edward's kinship to William was on the maternal side, not on that of the blood-royal of England: and as to Harold's oath, it was extorted by force and fraud, and was entirely *nil* in that it pledged Harold to do what he had no right to do,—the diversion of the crown from the will of the English people. William stormed and threatened, and, in building ships and organising troops, made active preparations for the invasion of England.

Harold set about preparations for the defence of his kingdom. He spent the summer in the south, getting ready a fleet and army. He had to wait too long for William; provisions falling short in the beginning of September, he had to disband the most of his troops. And meantime another foe, and this one of his own house, was intriguing against him—his brother Tostig. Harold had given Tostig the earldom of Northumberland; but he reigned so badly that the people rose and expelled him,—Harold sanctioning the expulsion. Tostig now went to Harold Hardrada, the King of Norway, and induced him to invade England. A fleet was sent up the Humber; York was captured, and there Harold Hardrada was proclaimed King. But English Harold—hastily getting an army together, met the invaders at Stamford Bridge; and there, on September 25th, a fierce battle was fought, —ending in victory for England; the Norwegian King and the traitorous Tostig both being slain.

But in meeting the Norwegian invasion, the Anglo-Saxons lost England. Four days later, William, with a banner consecrated by the Pope, landed near Pevensey in Sussex. Harold was seated at a banquet in York when the evil news reached him. And now, the last in a life of turmoil, Harold began his march through England; collecting on his way what troops he could, he reached the hill Senlac, nine miles from Hastings, on the 13th of October. Here he marshalled his army—nearly all on foot—and next day the Normans attacked him. It was a well-contested fight; but discipline and knighthood prevailed. The setting sun witnessed a routed English army, its leader slain, and the Norman William, conqueror of England.

The eleventh century, so momentous in English history, was also an important one in the history of Scotland. The Norse energy and ability to rule shewed itself in the Earls of Orkney, who dominated the Hebrides, and Ross, Moray, Sutherland, and Caithness. About 1010, Earl Sigurd married the daughter of King Malcolm II. In 1014, Sigurd went over to Ireland, to aid the Danish kings there against Brian Boru. In a battle at Clontarf, the Danes were defeated—Sigurd being slain—and the Celtic dynasty was restored. Sigurd's territories were divided amongst two sons by a former marriage, and an infant son, Thurfinn, by Malcolm's daughter; to the last was assigned the earldom of Caithness. In 1018—taking advantage of the distracted state of England in this, the first year of Canute's reign—Malcolm invaded upper Northumbria; by a victory at Carham, near Coldstream on the

Tweed, the Lothians were brought more under his rule. But after Canute's return from his pilgrimage to Rome, he invaded Scotland, and received the submission of Malcolm and two under-kings, Mælbæthe and Jehmarc.

Malcolm II. was succeeded by his grandson Duncan,—a daughter's son by a secular abbot of Dunkeld. Duncan's right was disputed by his cousin Thurfirm, who was now Earl of Orkney. Duncan went north to check the advance of his kinsman, and was defeated near the Pentland Firth. But an invasion of Danes under King Sweyn on the coast of Fife, and which was probably made in aid of Thurfirm, was defeated by Macbeth, an able general of Duncan's, and who, it is said, was also a grandson of Malcolm's, by another daughter. Duncan was *probably*—as in Shakespeare's great drama—killed by Macbeth. Certainly, to the exclusion of Duncan's two sons, Malcolm and Donaldbane, Macbeth seized the crown. He reigned seventeen years—1040 to 1057—being contemporary with the Confessor,— a glowing description of whom, posing as a saint with miraculous powers of healing, occurs in Shakespeare's play. When, on the return of Earl Godwin from exile, there was a general exodus of the Normans, whom Edward had placed in high positions, many of them went to Scotland, and were well received by Macbeth. He appears historically, in spite of our great poet's portraiture of him, to have been an able monarch; and he might be said to represent Celtic supremacy in Scotland, as against the tendency to subvert it by Anglo-Saxon alliances. Duncan had married the daughter of Siward, Earl of Northumbria, and Macbeth had to resist the attacks of Siward on behalf of his grandson Malcolm. Malcolm spent his boyhood in Cumbria, and his youth at the court of the Confessor. He appealed to Edward for help to gain his father's throne, and by an English army under Siward, and Macduff, the powerful Thane of Fife, and Tostig, the son of Earl Godwin, Macbeth was overthrown and slain.

Malcolm III., named Canmore—"big-head"—reigned thirty-five years, 1058 to 1093. The Norman victory at Hastings brought to the Scottish court, then at Dunfermline, a number of English refugees—these were a leaven of higher culture and refinement amongst the rude thanes and chieftains, and tended to further the advance of civilization, of letters and the arts of life, throughout the northern kingdom. And numbers of Normans also came and took service under Malcolm—and thus it came about that not only in England, but in Scotland also, most of the noble families have in them a strain of Norman blood.

Amongst the refugees were Edgar Atheling and his sisters, grand-children of Edmund Ironside. Malcolm married Margaret, the eldest sister; she was a noble woman, learned, pious, and charitable, doted upon by her husband, and ever influencing his fierce nature for good. Thus connected by birth with the heir of the old race of English Kings, Malcolm invaded Northumberland on behalf of Edgar; but William was too strong for him, and in turn invaded Scotland. William marched as far north as Abernethy, where he forced Malcolm to do him homage. William never really subjugated Northumbria north of the Tyne, but built Newcastle as a border fortress. After the death of William in 1087, Malcolm made other invasions of Northumbria, and to consolidate the possession of Lothian, he removed the seat of government to Edinburgh. In 1093, he made a desperate attempt to gain the counties of Northumberland and Cumberland; but, whilst besieging the border fortress of Alnwick, he was attacked, defeated, and killed by a Norman army.

The marriage of Henry, the youngest son of the Conqueror, with Matilda, daughter of Malcolm, and niece of Edgar Atheling, united the Norman and the older English royal lines. Henry's son William was, in 1120, drowned in "The White Ship," and his only other child, Maud, was thus the rightful heir to the throne. But the proud Norman barons had not been used to female rule; so, after Henry's death, in 1135, Stephen, a son of the Conqueror's daughter Adela, was made King.

David I., youngest son of Malcolm Canmore, succeeding his two elder brothers, was at this time King of Scotland, and he took up the cause of his niece Maud. In 1138 he invaded Northumberland, penetrating into Yorkshire. At Northallerton he was met and defeated in a battle called "Of the Standard." It is said that he was gaining the day, when an English soldier cut off the head of one of the slain, placed it on a spear, and called out that it was the head of the King of Scots, thus causing a panic in the Scottish army which the King, riding amongst it without his helmet, vainly tried to overcome. After peace, David was allowed to retain Northumberland and

Durham, excepting the fortresses of Newcastle and Bamborough. He was so good a king that after his death, in 1153, he was canonised.

David was succeeded by his twelve years old grandson, Malcolm. He was, from his gentle disposition, called *The Maiden*. He was greatly attached to the English King, Henry II., accompanying him to France as a volunteer in his army. Malcolm's Scottish subjects were afraid of the influence of the older sovereign. Homage rendered by the Scottish kings for their possessions in England, was always liable to be construed into national homage; and it was notified that Malcolm had gone beyond mere homage, and had absolutely resigned these possessions. So Malcolm had a strong message from Scotland, asking him to return; this he did, was again in favour with his people, but died in 1165, being then only twenty-four years old.

He was succeeded by his brother William. He was called *The Lion* because he used as his armorial bearing a red lion—*rampant*—that is in heraldry, standing upon its hind legs; and this has ever since been the heraldric cognizance of Scottish royalty. In 1174, for the recovery of his ancestral possessions in Northumberland, William invaded England. One day riding in a mist with a slender retinue, he came upon a body of four hundred English horse. At first he thought that this was a portion of his own army; seeing his mistake he fought boldly, but was overpowered and made prisoner. He was taken to Northampton and conducted into King Henry's presence, with his feet tied together under his horse's belly. Now Henry had just been to Canterbury doing penance at the tomb of the murdered Thomas à Becket; he had walked barefoot through the city, prostrated himself on the pavement before the shrine, passed the whole night in the church, and in the morning had himself scourged by the priests with knotted cords. And now, as a token that his penance had reconciled him to heaven, and obtained the saint's forgiveness, here was his enemy, the King of Scots, delivered into his hands.

Henry shewed no generosity towards his captive. He demanded to have homage paid him as Lord Paramount of Scotland. In his prison, first at Richmond, and then at Falaise in Normandy, William's spirit was so far broken that he acceded to Henry's demands, and the Scottish parliament, to obtain the release of their king, ratified a dishonourable treaty. At York the required homage was publicly paid; and for fifteen years it continued in full force. But in 1189, Henry's son, Richard, the Lion-hearted, on the eve of his crusade to the Holy Land,—desirous to place his home affairs in safety during his absence, renounced the claim of general homage extorted from William,—reserving only such homage as was anciently rendered by Malcolm Canmore.

And in almost unbroken peace between the two countries for upwards of a century, the generous conduct of Richard bore good fruit. Then a course of accidents, which nearly extinguished the Scottish royal family, gave an English monarch the opportunity for reviving old pretensions to supremacy, and was thus the cause of renewed wars and national animosities.

William died in 1214, and was succeeded by his son, Alexander III. He reigned thirty-five years, and being of good parts, and with considerable force of character, did much for the progress of Scotland in the arts of civilization. He was succeeded in 1249 by his son, Alexander III., then only eight years of age. He married the daughter of Henry III., but the children of the marriage died young. The chief trouble of his reign was from Norwegian invasions, but in 1263 Alexander defeated Haco, King of Norway, at Largs, at the mouth of the Firth of Clyde. By this victory Scotland obtained possession of the Hebrides and the Isle of Man. Alexander was accidentally killed in 1263; riding too near the edge of a cliff on the Fifeshire coast, near Kinghorn, in the dusk of the evening, his horse stumbled and threw him over the cliff.

How Scotland became a Free Nation.

WE are not attempting to present a detailed history of Scotland: such a history has both a general and a national value, and there has been no lack of writers of ability to give to it their best of thought and of research. But as having been a supreme crisis in this history, and as having placed Scotland high on the list of free nations, we give a brief summary of events at the end of the thirteenth and beginning of the fourteenth century.

The English King, Edward the First, who has been called the greatest of the Plantagenets, was led to undertake the conquest of Scotland. He found that insurgent spirits amongst his own subjects therein found refuge, and that France —the natural enemy of England—was generally in alliance with Scotland. His designs on Scotland had three separate phases. First: King Alexander the Third of Scotland having died without immediate issue, the crown devolved upon his grand-daughter, Margaret, daughter of

Eric, King of Norway. The young princess is called in history the Maid of Norway. Edward proposed a marriage between her and his own eldest son, also named Edward. A treaty for this marriage was entered into. It was one of the might-have-beens of history; had it taken place, and been fruitful, the union of the crowns might have been anticipated by over three centuries, and the after-histories of the two countries very different. But on her voyage to take possession of her crown, Margaret sickened; she landed at Orkney, and there died, September, 1290.

Then there were various claimants to the crown, the rights of the claimants dating back several generations. All having their partizans, and anarchy and conflict appearing imminent, it was agreed that Edward should be arbitrator. He here saw an opening for the revival of what might now have been thought the obsolete claim of the English sovereign to be recognised as Lord Paramount of Scotland. Two of the candidates, Robert Bruce, Lord of Annandale, and John Baliol, Lord of Galloway, were found to be nearer in blood to the throne than all the others. Both of them traced their descent from daughters of David, Earl of Huntingdon, brother of King William, called *The Lion*. Edward gave his decision in favour of Baliol, as being descended from the elder daughter; but he declared that the crown was to be held under him

EDWARD I.

as feudal superior; and Baliol did homage to Edward as to his lord sovereign, and was summoned as a peer to the English Parliament.

Edward soon shewed that his claim was not to be a merely formal one; he demanded the

F

surrender of three important Scottish fortresses. Baliol would himself have submitted to this arrogant demand, but at the instigation of the nobles he sent a refusal, and a formal renunciation of his vassalage. In a war which in 1294 broke out between France and England, Scotland allied itself with France. Then Edward assembled a powerful army and invaded Scotland. He gained a victory near Dunbar, and made a triumphant march through the Lowlands. The country was divided within itself; the powerful Bruce faction was arrayed against that of Baliol. Baliol made a cringing submission to Edward; and Bruce sued for the nominal throne, as tributary sovereign of Scotland. "Think'st thou I am to conquer a kingdom for thee?" was Edward's stern reply; and he forthwith took measures to make evident his purpose of keeping Scotland to himself. He appointed an English nobleman his viceroy, garrisoned the fortresses with English troops, and removed to London the regalia and the official records of the Kingdom, and also the legendary stone upon which the Scottish Kings had sat on their coronation. It was the very nadir in the cycle of Scottish history.

Then came revolts, with varied measures of

success. A notable hero, Sir William Wallace, whose name yet lives in Scottish hearts as the very incarnation of patriotism and courage, took the leadership in an all but successful insurrection. But the larger, better appointed, and better disciplined armies of Edward again placed Scotland under his iron heel. Brave Wallace was, through treachery, taken prisoner, carried up to London, and tried for treason at Westminster Hall. "I never could be a traitor to Edward, for I was never his subject," was Wallace's defence: the English judges condemned him to a traitor's death. With the indignities customary in these semi-barbarous times, he was executed on Tower Hill, 23rd August, 1305.

Robert Bruce, Earl of Carrick, a grandson of the Bruce who was Baliol's rival for the Crown, had been one of Wallace's ablest lieutenants. He had a fine person, was brave and strong, was moreover prudent and skilful, fitted to be a leader of men, both in the council and on the battle-field. He had the faults of his times—could be passionate, and in his passion cruel and relentless. He now aimed at the sovereignty, and within a year of the death of Wallace, had himself, with a miniature court and slender following, crowned

King at Scone. When Edward heard of this he was exceedingly wroth, and would himself again go into Scotland and stamp out all the embers of rebellion. In 1307, he did accompany an army through Cumberland, to within three miles of the Scottish border. But ruthless and determined in spirit, he was now old and feeble in body, and

> "Hate and fury ill-supplied
> The stream of life's exhausted tide."

He was stricken by mortal sickness and died, 6th July, 1307. Before he died he made his son promise to carry his unburied corpse with the army until Scotland was again fully conquered. The Second Edward did not carry out that savage injunction, but had his father buried in Westminster Abbey, where his tomb styles him, with greater truth than is found in many monumental inscriptions, " The hammer of Scotland."

For years Bruce was little other than a guerilla chief, sometimes even a fugitive, hiding in highland fastnesses, or in the Western Isles. He was under the pope's excommunication, for that in a quarrel within the walls of a consecrated church in Dumfries he had slain Sir John Comyn, who had also certain hereditary claims to the throne. But he was possessed of wonderful perseverance.

Edward II. had, by the withdrawal of his father's great army of invasion, encouraged the Scottish hopes of independence. In different parts of the country there were partial insurrections against English rule and English garrisons. In March, 1313, by a sudden *coup*, Edinburgh Castle was taken. Gradually the greater number of the Scottish nobles, with their retainers, declared for Bruce. By the early spring of 1314, all the important towns except Stirling had passed out of English possession; and it was to be given up unless relieved before midsummer.

Such a state of things would not have come about in the days of the elder Edward, before he would have been with an army in Scotland, to drive back the tide of insurrection. Now, instigated by his counsellors to save Stirling, Edward the Second assembled one of the largest armies which had ever been under the command of an English King. One hundred thousand men are said to have crossed the Scottish border, the flower of English chivalry—the best trained archers in the world—soldiers from France, Welsh and Irish, a mighty host. Bruce with all his efforts could not bring into the field more than one disciplined soldier for every three such in the enemy's ranks; but there were many loose camp-followers, half-armed and undisciplined, who, if their only aim was plunder, could yet harass and cut off stragglers of an army on the march. Bruce himself was a consummate general, possessing the entire confidence of his men; he had the choice of his ground, and he had as lieutenants his brave brother Edward, his nephew Randolph, and his faithful follower Lord James Douglas, all commanding men with whom they had in previous hard fights stood shoulder to shoulder and achieved victory.

On the afternoon of the 23rd of June, 1314, the mighty English host rolled on in splendid order, towards the plain near Stirling, where Bruce, taking every advantage of the ground, had posted his army. In the evening there were a few skirmishes, and the Bruce had a personal encounter with, and slew an English knight, De Bohun. Such an act—if it could have been honourably avoided—was not generalship, but in those days personal prowess in the field was an essential for leadership.

On the next morning, before daybreak, the battle began, it is named "of Bannockburn," from a small stream, the Bannock, on the right of

Bruce's position. We have no need to say that, despite of numbers and discipline being on the side of the English, and courage a common quality in both armies, it was a decisive Scottish victory. The causes of this result are not far to seek; Bruce was the better general, and he had a position from which he could bring a superior force to bear upon any single point of attack. The course of the English cavalry lay through morass and broken ground; and by pitfalls and barriers, Bruce had made this ground more difficult and dangerous. He closed at the earliest possible moment with those terrible foes at a distance—the English archers; his object was to throw the enemy into confusion at some one point, knowing how such confusion spreads itself. The very numbers of the English told against their united action—more than the half of them were never actually engaged in the fight. And when some early advantages showed in favour of the Scots, their motley crowd of camp followers thought that victory was assured, and, eager for plunder and revenge, they burst down the slopes with wild shouts and gesticulations. And thus a partial confusion in the English ranks became a general panic, a rout, and a "save-himself-who-can " flight from the field. With the Douglas in hot pursuit, Edward rode across the country to Dunbar, where he found a small vessel by which he sailed to England.

And thus—by one day's devoted patriotism, by steady valour and skilful generalship, as Scottish historians say,—by hap-hazard, stratagem, and surprise, as others have alleged, Robert Bruce secured his crown, and could now really be called *Rex Scotorum*, King of Scots. And Scotland itself rose, by that day's event, from the dust of conquest and depression into a free and independant state, to be governed by its own laws and ruled by its own princes. There have been since that day some disastrous Scottish defeats by English arms, and Scotland has often felt itself in the shadow of a superior power; but the halo of Bannockburn has never been obscured. It was not only a glorious day for Scotland, but an auspicious one for England also; the Scottish people could, after a preliminary union of the two crowns in a sovereign common to both countries, frankly, and on equal terms, join with England in a national union; together, hand in hand, going down the stream of history; in weal and in woe standing by and aiding each other.

Scotland in the Two Hundred Years following Bannockburn.

NEVER in all its previous history had Scotland been so united within itself, or held so important a place amongst other nations, as during the reign of Robert Bruce.

In what are called the dark ages of Europe, feudalism was a general institution amongst the western nations. The Conqueror introduced this phase of society into England; and it soon thereafter spread into Scotland, where clanship had been its forerunner. Under the feudal system, the King was chief; the land of the nation was nominally his, to bestow in large estates on the nobles and great barons; these became his vassals, under tenure obligations to do him homage, to take part, with their retainers, in his wars, and to attend and take part in the Great Councils which he summoned. The lesser barons, or fief-holders met in their districts or shires, and chose from amongst themselves deputies or representatives. And the Great

Council contained besides, representatives of the clergy, and of the chartered boroughs. In England the national Council was divided into two separate houses, namely, that of Peers, where the members sat by personal right, and that of Commons, who were members by representation. In Scotland there was a single house : nobles and prelates, representatives of shires, and delegates from boroughs, all sat together, took a common share in the debates, and all votes were of equal account. Acts were made into law, and powers were granted for raising money, by the bills passed in Parliament, being assented to by the sovereign. The form of assent was touching the bills with the sceptre.

And the old Scottish statute book is replete with wise, well-considered laws. But from the powers assumed by the nobles, each virtually claiming absolute authority within his own domains, the administration was woefully defective. The nobles were, moreover, often engaged in deadly feuds against each other; perpetuating family quarrels through generations, and at times powerful houses would coalesce against sovereignty itself.

In the English quarrels which arose, a Scottish

army would be composed of brave and hardy fighting men, trained to arms, and devoted to their immediate leaders. But the leaders were jealous of, and many of them inimical to each other; so could not act in concert, and a battle under such circumstances would be a disaster and a disgrace. A great personality, like that of Robert the Bruce, could over-master the discordant elements, and make his own authority paramount; but amongst his successors there were several weak monarchs, unable to beat down personal rancour and ambition in the council and in the camp. And one great curse to Scotland in the fourteenth, fifteenth, and sixteenth centuries, was the comparatively large number of regencies, from the under ages of monarchs at their accession to the throne,—thus creating jealousy, rivalry, and partizanship amongst the more powerful nobles.

The burghs had risen in population and importance, generally clustering round the larger religious houses. Men not connected with the land either as proprietors or retainers, congregated together for mutual trade and mutual protection. The sovereigns encouraged this growth, as affording a readier means of raising revenue, and as an equipoise to the power of the nobles; granting the towns chartered privileges, which constituted them royal burghs. The citizens elected their municipal Council; the chief magistrate was styled Provost, the others Bailies. Many burghs were defended by walling, and the citizens were trained to arms; they had to defend the burgh, and, in levies, to help the King in his wars.

In the midland shires law and order obtained generally, but in the Highlands and their adjacent islands, and in the frontier shires, there was, as a rule, lawlessness and disorder. The halo of romance, largely kindled by the genius of Sir Walter Scott, hovers round the Scottish Highlands. The

"Land of green heath and shaggy wood,
Land of the mountain and the flood"

bred a stalwart race of brave men, with persistent loyalty in their hearts to their clanship, and to the hills and glens which were to them their fatherland; but they long continued in semi-barbarism, separated by race and language from the comparatively civilized Lowlands, with little of national patriotism, and a great distrust of the —to them distant—sovereignty of Holyrood.

They often, as did their forefathers in the time of the Romans, a thousand years previously, made plundering incursions into the Lowlands; but they had continual clan-quarrels amongst themselves, which helped to keep them in their native wilds, and the government would foment these quarrels, and even, to their mutual destruction, employ one clan against another. So late as the reign of James IV. an Act of Parliament, for the better government of the Highlands and Islands, states that for want of justices and sheriffs, these districts had become almost savage.

And the border counties—on both sides of the hardly defined line of demarcation—were also in an unsettled state. They, too, had their family clanships, their hereditary feuds, their predatory raids. There was a sort of debatable land of moor, forest, and morass, where neither national nor forest-law was paramount. On both sides Wardens of the marches were appointed, with a mutual understanding to prevent border-raiding. But the Wardens themselves were generally heads of the great neighbouring families, and they often broke their own laws, by sheltering or encouraging offenders. Altogether the picture which we gather from the history of Scotland in the fourteenth and fifteenth centuries is not a pleasant one to dwell upon.

But there were rifts in the cloud. The first James, 1406 to 1437, has left a noble record as a man of knightly nature, a fine poet, and a wise ruler. When eleven years of age, he was put by his father, Robert III., on board of a vessel to sail to France, to save him from his uncle, the Duke of Albany, who had caused the death by starvation of his elder brother. The vessel was captured by the English, and the young prince was for eighteen years a prisoner. But he was well educated, and seems to have had great freedom of movement—even taking part in the French wars. He married Joan Beaufort, daughter of the Earl of Somerset, and nearly related to the royal family of England. In 1424, a ransom was negotiated; James was set at liberty, and he and his queen were crowned at Scone. Under him many wise laws were enacted for the proper administration of justice, and for the fostering of home trade and foreign commerce. His great task was in curtailing the powers assumed by the nobles. This made him enemies, and cost him his life. Temporarily occupying a house in Perth, a band of miscreants under Sir Robert Graham, who had recently been punished by the King for law-breaking, burst at night into the King's chamber, and in his wife's presence savagely slew him. The Queen took wild vengeance on the murderers.

The Older Scottish Literature.

PERHAPS in no part of Scotland was there —even in the fourteenth century—pure Anglo-Saxon blood. The Lothians and the south-eastern shires had been a portion of the old kingdom of Northumbria, in which, with the Angles as a normal population, there had been large Danish settlements; and numbers of Normans also settled therein, both before and after the Conquest; whilst the descendants of the old Britons had peopled the south-western shires, from the Solway to the Clyde. Thus whilst the generally spoken language of the two countries was essentially the same, the literature of England would be more purely Teutonic; that of Scotland would include Celtic elements; but these elements would assert themselves more in qualifying the style of the literature than in the use of Celtic words.

Thus, Scottish poetry generally shows a passionate love of Nature; its picturesque descriptions and vivid colourings reaching or bordering upon exaggeration. Its humour is broad, and of coarsish fibre. And then the sentiment of patriotism has ever been more pronounced in Scotland than in England. As a rule, English Nationalism was, after the Norman Conquest, even in the most disastrous times, safe and self-assertive. On the other hand, Scottish Nationalism was at one period, for a time, entirely lost; it was often in extreme danger, and was saved only by extreme efforts,—as we might say, "by the skin of the teeth." Can we wonder then that fervid patriotism pervades,—becomes obtrusive even, in Scottish literature; and that this literature almost deifies the National heroes?

Thus, amongst the earlier efforts in Scottish poetry replete with this glowing patriotism, we have Archbishop Barbour's poem, *The Bruce;* Blind Harry's *History of Sir William Wallace;* and Andrew of Wyntoun's *Chronykil of Scotland.* We mentioned as a poet James I., he wrote *The King's Quhair* (*i.e.*, book); it is in Chaucer's seven-line stanza, and contains the best poetry published in Great Britain, between that of Chaucer and the Elizabethan period. From a full heart he tells the story of his love; a love which brightened his life, and shone true at his death, when his queen did her best to save him from the daggers of the conspirators. The King,—whilst a prisoner in Windsor Castle,—saw from his window his future queen, walking in an adjacent garden.

> "Cast I down mine eyes again,
> Where as I saw, walking under the tower,
> Full secretly, now comen here to plain.
> The fairest, or the freshest younge flower
> That ever I saw, methought, before that hour,
> For which, sudden abate—anon astart—
> The blood of all my body to my heart.
>
> "And in my head I drew right hastily
> And eftesoons I leant it out again,
> And saw her walk that very womanly,
> With no wight mo', but only women twain,
> Then gan I study to myself, and sayn,—
> 'Ah, sweet! are ye a worldly creature,
> Or heavenly thing in likeness of nature?
>
> "'Or, are ye god Cupidis own princess
> And comin are to loose me out of hand?
> Or, are ye very Nature the goddess,
> That have depainted with your heavenly hand
> This garden full of flowers as they stand?
> What shall I think, alas! what reverence
> Shall I outpour unto your excellence?'"

Another king, James Fifth of the name, was also a poet; he may be called the originator of that satirical humour in verse which afterwards characterized so many Scottish poets, including Robert Burns, the greatest of them all.

After the union of the crowns, and the removal of the Scottish Court to London, in 1603, the old language came to be considered a provincial

WILLIAM DRUMMOND.

dialect. William Drummond, of Hawthornden (1585-1649), was the first notable Scottish poet who wrote well in modern English. He was imbued with true literary taste and feeling, and he ranks, as do subsequent Scottish writers, amongst British authors.

The Lowland folk-speech has really changed less from the Old English than the tongue of any other portion of the island; its glossary is very largely a key to Chaucer and Spenser, to Barbour and Andrew Wyntoun. As might have been expected, the folk-speech which is nearest to the English of modern literature is that of the more remote Highlands, as of Inverness and its surroundings. Where the old Gaelic has succumbed to book-learned English, there was no intermediate stage of the older tongue.

That the Scottish tongue is a fitting vehicle for pathos as well as for humour, scores of fine old songs are in evidence. Allan Ramsay's *Gentle Shepherd*, a pastoral drama of the loves and lives of the Scottish peasantry in the beginning of the last century, is the best lengthy example we have of every-day folk-speech. Burns never hesitated, when it seemed to better suit his verse or his meaning, to introduce modern English words; Ramsay rarely does this. With Burns the Scottish dialect as the expression of high-class poetry, might well have ended; but it yet lingers on, chiefly in humorous songs and descriptions.

The Reformation in England and in Scotland.

IN the progress of civilization, the middle of the sixteenth century may be taken as the turning point between the old past, with its feudalism, its authoritative church, its restricted culture, its antiquated science,—and the newer order of things from which has sprung the ever-expanding present. Since Guttenberg first used moveable types, a century had so far perfected his invention that books were becoming plentiful; and the one which is morally and socially, as well as religiously, the chief book in the world, had been translated into the mother-tongue of England. Towns were asserting their chartered privileges. The telescope was ransacking the heavens, and, for the first time, Magellan had circumnavigated the globe. Cannon were used in warfare, and iron had been smelted in England. The newspaper had been born; and Law was gradually gaining the ascendancy over disorder and old prerogative.

The Reformation of religion had established itself in Central and Northern Europe, and was now fighting its way in England and Scotland. But the battle with Papal authority and its dogmatic creeds was begun under very different circumstances, was carried on by very different methods, and had very different results in the two neighbouring countries.

How did the English Reformation come about? During nearly forty years in the first half of the sixteenth century (1509 to 1547) England was ruled by the last of her really despotic kings, Henry VIII. As everybody knows, Henry had a peculiar domestic experience,—he married in succession six wives. As fresh fancies took him, he rid himself of four of these—two by divorce, and two by the headsman's axe. One wife, Jane Seymour, died in childbirth of his only son, who succeeded him as Edward VI. Wife No. 6, by her extraordinary prudence contrived to escape destruction, and survived the kingly monster. *This* is a harsh term for the historical father of the English church, and some modern historians of ability and repute have done their best—as has been done in the cases of Macbeth and Richard III., as these kings are portrayed by Shakespeare

—to partially whitewash Henry. That he was, in common parlance, a great king, and a man of ability, of energy and decision, and that under him England prospered, and held an advanced position amongst the nations, few will dispute; but that he was a cruel, lustful, selfish tyrant seems equally undeniable. He made use of men and women as subservient to his will or his pleasure, and when his ends were so served, he ruthlessly destroyed them. His great minister, Wolsey, would not bend to his wishes in the matter of divorcing his first wife, so Wolsey was degraded, and in his old age sent into seclusion, to die of a broken heart. And in succession Thomas Cromwell, Sir Thomas More, and the Earl of Surrey, suffered the fate of Anne Boleyn and Catherine Howard.

Henry, when a young man, opposed the Reformation. He wrote a book against Luther and his heresies, which so pleased the Pope that he granted Henry the title of *Defender of the Faith*. This papal title has passed down by inheritance through all succeeding English sovereigns; every coin from the mintage of Queen Victoria bears its initial letters.

Henry first married, under the Pope's dispensation, the widow of his elder brother Arthur, Catherine of Arragon, by whom he had a daughter, afterwards Queen Mary. But the King fell in love—if, in the passions of such a man, the noble word *love* can be rightly used—with Anne Boleyn, one of Catherine's lady attendants. To gain Anne, Henry, after a number of years of wedded life with Catherine, all at once became conscience-stricken that his marriage with her was an unlawful one; and he asked the Pope to recall his dispensation and annul the marriage. Now, Catherine was sister to the Emperor of Germany, Charles the Fifth, one of the Pope's best supporters in these sad Reformation times. And, moreover, to have rescinded the dispensation would have been an admission of papal fallibility; so the Pope gave Henry a refusal.

Henry threw off his allegiance to the Pope, and had himself acknowledged by Parliament as the supreme head of the English Church. Powerful, unscrupulous, and popular, he confiscated church revenues, broke up monasteries, and by Act of Parliament, in 1537, completed politically the English Reformation. It was, so far as the King was concerned, a reformation only in name, for as to liberty of conscience, and the right of private judgment, he was as arrogant a bigot as any pope who ever wore the tiara. He vacillated in his own opinions, but enforced those he held at the time by such severe enactments, that many persons of both religions were burned as heretics.

And from the Anglican Church, so founded on despotism and intolerance, can we wonder that the shadow of Rome has never been thoroughly lifted? In the abstract it is essentially a close corporation of ecclesiastics, the mere people hardly counting as a necessary factor. Its sacraments have still miraculous or supernatural properties attached to them; no one must officiate therein who has not been *ordained*, and the assumed powers of ordination came through the Romish Church. From the older Church it adopted certain creeds, as dogmatic in their assertions, and intolerant in their fulminations, as were ever Papal Bulls or Decrees of Councils. Of course the mellowing influence of time, the broadening thoughts of later years, and the rivalship of Nonconformity, have done much to take out old stings and deaden old intolerance; whilst a cloud of witnesses for righteousness and progress in the Church itself, have raised it above its old self, and brought it in nearer touch with the spirit of the present age.

The history of the Scottish Reformation is an entirely different one. Instead of being originated and fostered by State authority, it was a fierce and obstinate battle with such authority. Scotland was then under one of its disastrous regencies, that of Mary of Guise, the widow of King James V., acting for her infant daughter Mary, known afterwards in history as the beautiful and unfortunate Queen of Scots. The Reformation in England had sent a wave of agitation into Scotland, and this wave advanced strongly as refugees from the cruel persecutions of Mary Tudor flocked into the Northern Kingdom; and as the Regent, with her coadjutor, the bigoted and relentless Cardinal Beaton, also began to persecute the new faith, and send its adherents to the stake; for it has ever been found to be a true saying, "The blood of the martyrs is the seed of the Church." In revenge for the burning, in 1545, of one of the saintliest of men, George Wishart, a party of the Reformers murdered the Cardinal in his own castle of St. Andrews, from one of the windows of which he had gloated over the martyr's cruel death.

In 1557, a number of the Reformers, including several noblemen, and styling themselves the Lords of the Congregation, entered into a mutual bond or covenant, "To defend the whole congregation of Christ against Satan and all his powers; to have prayers made and the sacraments administered in the vulgar tongue; in worship to use only the Bible, and the Prayer-book of Edward VI." In 1559, the Regent, who was entirely under French influence, and had been gradually filling high offices with Frenchmen, and accumulating French troops, issued a proclamation, forbidding any one to preach or administer the sacraments without the authority of the bishops.

And at this period a sterling man fitted to be a leader in such turbulent times, John Knox, appears in the forefront of the conflict. He had been college-bred, and became a priest, but adopted the Reformation in its Calvinistic phase, and, as he had opportunity, disseminated the new tenets with eloquence and zeal. After Beaton's death, his slayers, with others, and Knox amongst these, held out the castle of St. Andrews for fourteen months, but had to yield at last to their French besiegers, and were sent prisoners to France. Knox had to work in the galleys on the river Loire. But again he is in Scotland, preaching from place to place. After a powerful sermon against idolatry in a church in Perth, a priest began to celebrate mass. Heated by the glowing words of Knox, the people broke the images in the church. The Regent was very wroth, she deposed the Protestant provost of the city, and threatened it with French troops. The Congregation raised troops and appealed to Elizabeth, now on the English throne, for aid. Elizabeth sent some troops, and there was fighting with varied successes, until, by a treaty made in Edinburgh, the French agreed to abandon Scotland, and the Protestants were to be allowed the free exercise of their religion. In the Scottish Parliament of 1560 there was a solemn abjuration of the Pope and the mass. And the Geneva Confession of Faith was constituted the theological standard of the kingdom.

Differing from the English Church with its orders, its episcopacy, and its sovereign headship, the Scottish Reformers denied the authority of the sovereign, or secular government, to interfere in the affairs of the Church; determining that these affairs should be under the direction of a Court of Delegates, the greater number being chosen from the ministers, all of whom were of the same standing and dignity,

JOHN KNOX.

and the remainder—with equal authority in the deliberations—of a certain number of the laity, called Elders, thus forming what is called "The General Assembly of the Church." The sacraments were to be simple observances, spiritual only as they were spiritually received. Church edifices were regarded as merely stone and lime structures, having no claims to special regard, except during divine service. So to these Reformers, defacing in the churches what had been considered sacred statuary and ornamentation, even to the sign of the cross, was deemed a ready mode of testifying against Popish superstitions. As to the abbeys and monasteries—"Pull down the nests," said stern John Knox, "and the rooks will fly away."

Thus the Kirk of Scotland was essentially democratic in its origin, and, although always rigid and often intolerant, it has in the main so continued. Its theological tenets, although wordy and abstruse, were a whetstone to the intellect, and helped to develope a serious and thoughtful, a reading, and an argumentative people. Shepherds meeting each other on the hillsides, weavers with their yarn at the village beetling-stone, would, like Milton's angels :—

> "Reason high
> Of providence, foreknowledge, will, and fate,
> Fixed fate, free-will, foreknowledge absolute."

The English Church, on the other hand, did not encourage doctrinal discussion, but simple faith in its articles, and obedience to its rubric.

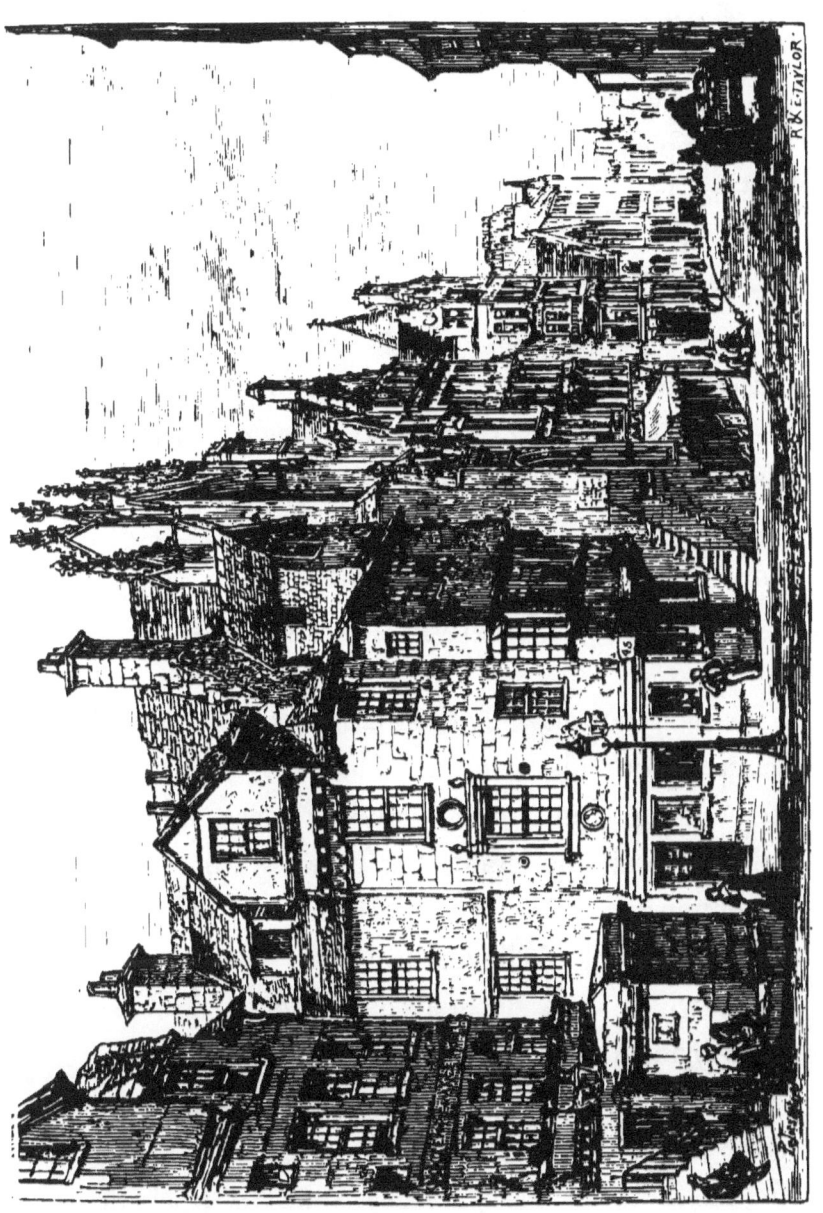

JOHN KNOX'S HOUSE.

But—which we would hardly have expected from its complex system of faith, and its niceties in phraseology—the Presbyterian Kirk produced zeal and earnest devotedness in the Scottish people. Without ordination by a bishop, whose orders were presumed to have come in direct succession from the Apostles, the ministers were held in high reverence and esteem; without printed prayers its common members learned to pray. It had its army of martyrs; except amongst Puritan Nonconformists, the Scottish Covenanters have hardly their English representatives.

John Knox largely impressed the Reformed Church with his own individuality. No doubt he was rigid, and, to our modern ideas, narrow-minded and intolerant. He would not have accomplished the work he did if he had not himself thoroughly believed in it, as the greatest work which then needed to be done. He has been blamed for speaking harsh words to Queen Mary; but he had to speak what he felt to be stern truths, for which honied words could hardly fit themselves. Mary, accustomed to fascinate the eyes and sway the wills of all who approached her, demanded of Knox:—"Who are you who

THE REFORMATION. 97

dare dictate to the sovereign and nobles of this realm?" "I am, Madam," answered Knox, "a subject of this realm." A subject, and therefore

JOHN KNOX'S PULPIT, ST. GILES'S.
(From the Scottish Antiquarian Museum.)

a co-partner in the realm; to the fullest extent of his knowledge and his capabilities responsible for its right government; just as the Hebrew prophets

H

claimed a right to stand before their kings, and, not always in smooth words, to denounce sin and hypocrisy, oppression, and backslidings from the law of God.

For supporting the introduction of bishops into the Presbyterian Church, as impairing the republican equality of its ministers, Knox had bitterly rebuked the Regent Morton. But when, in November, 1572, the Regent stood by the grave of the Reformer, it was in a choking voice that he pronounced the grand eulogium :—" There lies he, who never feared the face of man."

At the era of the Reformation no translation of the Scriptures had yet been printed in Scotland ; what copies in the vernacular had been brought from England, were in the hands of the wealthy ; indeed few of the common people could then have read them. The parish school as yet was not. The old church had not encouraged inquiry into the rationale of its dogmas, and although theological discussion was in the air, it had not penetrated into the lower strata of Scottish society. And thus the popular outburst against the old church was hardly founded on conscience and conviction ; in its beginnings at least, it was more a revolution against priestly domination.

THE REFORMATION.

But the cry of *idolatry* was raised. In the destruction of images in the churches, the leading reformers found the populace only too willing agents. Even architectural ornamentation—without religious significance—was removed or destroyed, the capitals of pillars were covered with plaster, the very tombs were rifled and defaced. The parish church had been the nucleus

GRAVE OF JOHN KNOX.

around which, for centuries, the veneration and the spiritual thought of past times had revolved, and now the idea of its "consecration" was to be banished from the popular mind. The reformers encouraged male worshippers to enter churches with their hats on—uncovering during prayer, psalm-singing, and scripture reading, and resuming their hats when the minister gave out the text for his sermon. When the discourse touched a popular chord, there was applause by clapping of hands and stamping of feet. Rome had demanded unquestioning submission to its authority,—an unreserved veneration for its ritual; and in breaking away from this bondage, the spirit of reverence was largely impaired.

Thus to other religionists, the form of worship in a Scottish church appeared bald and careless, hardly decorous. There was no private prayer on sitting down; in the public prayers, the stubborn presbyterian knee did not bend,—all stood upright, and the eyes would roam all over the church. In singing the psalms, there was no assistance from the swelling tones of an organ; gloves were put on during the benediction, and all were prepared for a hurried exit at its *Amen*. Funeral sermons, and even tomb-stones, were proscribed by the early reformers. One in King James's English retinue, accompanying him in a visit to Scotland, remarked,—"The Scots christen without the sign of the cross; they marry without the ring; and bury without any funeral service."

Although the old psalmist said,—"O sing unto the Lord a new song,"—the Presbyterians did not seem to think that anything had occurred in the following two thousand years, to incite to new songs of praise and thanksgiving: so they continued to sing only the Hebrew psalms. It was not until 1745 that the General Assembly authorized the use of Paraphrases,—that is, metrical versions of other portions of Scripture, but many congregations refused them. Now, there are authorized hymnals—the organ is again finding its place in the churches—and other changes have come about, bringing the form of service in nearer consonance with that of other churches, and with the more ornate tendency of the present times.

The Rival Queens—Mary and Elizabeth.

MARY'S evil fortunes began with her birth. Her dying father, heart-broken over a disastrous battle, lived only a week after his "poor lass," as he called her, was born. Then Henry VIII. of England saw in this infant niece of his a means of uniting the two crowns, much in the way by which a wolf unites itself with the lamb it devours, by having a marriage contracted between her and his only son, Prince Edward. He sent negotiators to enforce, under threats, his project. There was much opposition amongst the Scottish nobility. It looked like surrendering their country to England. They said to Henry's negotiators, "If your lad were a lass, and our lass were a lad, would you then be so earnest in this matter; and could you be content that our lad should, by marrying your lass, become King of England? No! your nation would never agree to have a Scot for King; and we will not have an Englishman as our King. And tho' the whole nobility of the realm should consent thereto, yet the common people would rebel against it; the very boys would hurl stones, and the wives handle their distaffs against it."

Henry was wroth exceedingly, threatened war, and demanded the custody of the child-Queen. To have him for an ally against the Queen-Regent and her minister, the persecutor Beaton, the Reformers temporized, and the Scottish Parliament consented to the match; Mary to be sent to Henry when she was ten years old.

In the meantime Henry got embroiled with France; and Scotland, under the influence of the Queen-Regent, allied itself with that country. Henry sent an army into Scotland. There were some Scottish successes; but at Pinkie, in 1547, the English general Somerset gained a complete victory. Before this event Henry had died; but his long cherished object, the possession of the child of Scotland, was still pressed, and now seemed on the point of attainment. But the Scottish people were irritated and alarmed to such a degree that they resolved to make the projected marriage impossible, by marrying their young mistress to the Dauphin of France, and sending her to be brought up at the French court. To this resolve Parliament gave a hasty assent; and in July 1548, the poor child, now in her sixth year, accompanied by her four Maries—girls her own age, of noble birth, her present play-fellows and future companions—was shipped off to France.

Prince Edward, who succeeded Henry as Edward VI., was twelve years of age when his father died, and he reigned only four years. Then there was the painful incident of Lady Jane Grey being pushed forward by her ambitious kindred as a claimant to the throne; the venture being death to her and to them. And then Henry's daughter by his first wife became Queen. A rigid Catholic, she at once took steps, intolerant, relentless, and cruel, to re-establish the old faith. The savage persecutions of her reign have rendered it for ever infamous. She goes down through all time as the *Bloody* Mary. Smithfield blazed with the fires of martyrdom; five Protestant bishops were amongst the sufferers. Happily her reign was a brief one, lasting only five years; and they were for her years of domestic misery, her marriage with the Spanish King, Philip II., being an unhappy and unfruitful one.

Her half-sister Elizabeth, the issue of Henry's

marriage with Anne Boleyn, succeeded to the throne in 1558. Elizabeth had been brought up as a Protestant, had been kept a close prisoner during Mary's reign,—narrowly escaping being herself a martyr. And now to maintain her claims to the throne, she had to depend upon her Protestant subjects; for the Catholics denied the validity of her father and mother's marriage, and consequently denied her legitimacy and right to reign. They asserted that Mary Stuart of Scotland was the rightful heir, and as such entitled to their allegiance.

A brief explanation will show on what foundation the Stuart claim—afterwards allowed at the death of Elizabeth in favour of Mary's son James—was based. At Bosworth Field, Richard III., of the house of York, was defeated and slain. The victor was Richmond of Lancaster, who thus became King Henry VII.; his son was Henry VIII., and his daughter Margaret married James IV., King of Scotland. The neighbouring Kings, James and Henry VIII., were thus brothers-in-law; none the less did they quarrel and go to war with each other, their hostilities ending, so far as James was concerned, with the battle of Flodden. Henry was then engaged in a war with France, and James was killed in the battle which his vanity had provoked, and which he generalled so badly. His son, James V., was Henry's nephew, and full cousin to Henry's children, Edward, Mary, and Elizabeth. Thus, failing direct legitimate heirs to the English throne, James's daughter Mary was, in virtue of her descent as the grand-daughter of Henry VII., the nearest heir.

At Elizabeth's accession, in 1558, Mary was sixteen years of age. As the wife of the Dauphin of France, the French monarchy put forward her claims as the rightful sovereign of England, and even had a coinage struck with her effigy thus designated. So Elizabeth feared and hated Mary as her rival; hated her yet more, with a woman's spite, for her beauty and accomplishments. Soon Mary, by his early death, lost her husband, then King of France, and at nineteen years of age, in the splendour of her queenly beauty, she—regretfully for the land of her youth —returned to her native Scotland.

By her sweet presence, her courtesy, and winning manners, Mary largely gained the hearts of her people; but murmurings soon arose about her foreign ways, her foreign favouritisms, and her fidelity to her Catholic faith. And a cloud gathered over her domestic life. She had married a young nobleman, Henry Stuart, Lord Darnley. He was next to Mary in the hereditary line of

MARY, QUEEN OF SCOTLAND.
(From a painting by Zucchero.)

succession to the English throne—as Mary was a grand-daughter of Margaret Tudor he was a grandson—by Margaret's second marriage with the Earl of Angus. He was also a Catholic. Darnley seems to have been little other than a handsome, but petulant, ill-behaved, and ill-mannered boy, fitted, neither by intellect nor disposition, to be the husband and life-companion of such a proud, clever, and accomplished woman as Mary. Mary refused him the crown-matrimonial, and they very soon fell apart. Mary was not forbidden to have her private chapel; an Italian singer in this chapel, David Rizzio, became a favourite, he acted as her secretary, and was admitted into the inner circle of Holyrood. One evening the supper-party was broken in upon by Darnley and a number of his associates, and Rizzio was dragged out to the landing, and by several weapons barbarously stabbed to death. Mary's fair countenance and gentle voice were mated with an iron will, persistent in carrying out her hatreds to the death. Darnley was murdered by a rude villain, Earl Bothwell, and Mary has never been satisfactorily cleared of complicity in the murder. Shortly afterwards she married this Bothwell—by force, her apologists say.

We shall not even briefly go over the oft-told tale of Mary's after-life. As the incidents loom out of the tangled web, we feel, even through the centuries, as if we would fain arrest them by a warning voice, fain save that fascinating woman from her doom. We feel a yearning pity, almost akin to love, although stern justice gives her blame as a woman, a wife, and a Queen. That pitiful winter's morning in Fotheringay Castle, in 1587, brought to Mary, by the headsman's axe, a cruel death, but also a kind release from captivity and unrest.

And what of her rival queen and kinswoman, "that bright Occidental star," Elizabeth? A woman with a strong masculine intellect, of dauntless courage, one fitted to rule and govern, and advance a nation. But unmistakably her father's daughter, cruel, heartless, unforgiving, and thoroughly false: with a woman's caprice exalting to supreme favouritism to-day, and striking down into the dust to-morrow. She signed Mary's death-warrant, and, by grimaces and plainest hints, she made her people slay her own cousin. And when the deed was irretrievably done she went into a hypocritical paroxysm of well-acted anger and regret, and dealt round punishment for the act which she herself had compassed. These two women cited to the bar of judgment, Mary might well hide her face for many sins and frailties; but the better actor would try to stand up, boldly and unabashed. Our own hearts must answer which of the two we justify, rather than the other.

Old Edinburgh.

> "Edina! Scotia's darling seat!
>   All hail thy palaces and tow'rs,
> Where once beneath a monarch's feet
>   Sat legislation's sov'reign powers!
>
> There, watching high for war's alarms,
>   Thy rough, rude fortress gleams afar;
> Like some bold vet'ran grey in arms,
>   And marked with many a seamy scar."

SO sang Burns, when "from marking wild-flowers on the banks of Ayr," he "sheltered," and was feted and petted in the "honoured shade" of the capital of Scotland. And Sir Walter Scott, in describing Marmion's approach to the city on a summer's morning, cannot, from a full proud heart, refrain from introducing his own personality:—

> "Such dusky grandeur clothed the height
>   Where the huge castle holds its state,
>   And all the steep slope down,
>   Whose ridgy back heaves to the sky,
>   Pil'd deep and massy, close and high—
>   Mine own romantic town!"

Doubtless, as a picturesque town, Edinburgh

stands in the foremost rank. The natural configuration of the ground in ridges and hollows, and the commanding prospects from its heights of undulating landscape, of broad Frith, of distant hills, and of the adjacent Arthur's Seat, like a couchant lion guarding the town, are striking, and stir up any poetic feeling that may be lurking in the heart. In the architecture there is a strange and incongruous mingling of the modern and the antique, of the genuine and the meretricious. There are many interesting historical memorials, and very many reminders of the everyday present. Buildings and monuments bring cherished and illustrious names to our mind; other names are obtruded which we would gladly forget. But no one can, from the Castle bastions, see the panorama of the city and its surroundings, without intense interest, and an admiration which will abide in the memory.

In 647, Edwin, the son of Ella, Saxon King of Northumbria, extended his conquests beyond the Forth. He re-fortified the rock-castle, called Puellerum, and to the little town which rose up around it, was given the name of Edwinsburgh. In 1128, Edinburgh was made a Royal burgh by David I. In 1215, a Parliament of Alexander II. met here for the first time. In 1296, the title of the chief magistrate was changed from Alderman to Provost.

In 1424, James I. was, at £40,000, ransomed from his long and unjust imprisonment in England: the towns of Edinburgh, Aberdeen, Perth, and Dundee, guaranteeing the ransom. James had, on his parole, been free to move about England; and he soon saw how far behind her his own land was in agriculture and commerce. To amend this he made laws, which to us seem meddlesome and going into petty details, but doubtless were then useful and progressive. For the prevention of fires in buildings it was advisable to enact that "hempe, lint and straw be not put in houses aboone or near fires," and that "nae licht be fetched from ane house to ane uther but within covered weshel or lanterne." The lofty piles of buildings, for which the older town of Edinburgh is now remarkable, were in the fifteenth century represented by wooden houses not exceeding two stories in height; for we find that in providing against fires, Parliament ordained that "at the common cost aucht twenty-fute ladders be made, and kept in a ready place in the town, for that use and none other." From the murder of James I. in Perth, in 1456, Edinburgh dates as the capital, and where Parliaments were exclusively held.

In 1496, in order to qualify the eldest sons of barons and freeholders for exercising the functions of sheriffs (holding judicial powers in a Scottish county) and ordinary justices, it was enacted that such be sent to grammar schools, and there remain, "quhill they be competentlie founded and have perfite Latin; and thereafter to remain three zeirs at the schules of art and jure; so that they may have knowledge and onderstanding of the laws." The population of Edinburgh was then about 8,000.

When, in 1503, Margaret, daughter of Henry VII., came to Scotland as the bride of James IV., the King met her at Dalkeith, and the royal lovers made their entry into Edinburgh, "the Kyng riding on a pallafroy, with the princesse behind him, and so through the toun." Ten years later came, on the 10th September, the sad news of Flodden, fought on the previous day; when the brave but fool-hardy King, and the flower of Scottish manhood "were a' wede away." At first it was consternation and the confusion of despair; but soon order and new energy prevailed.

Under pains of forfeiture of life and goods, all citizens capable of bearing arms were convoked to form, with the stragglers from Flodden, a fresh army: the older citizens were to defend the city. The women were, under a threat of banishment, forbidden to cry and clamour in the streets; the better sort were to go to church and pray for their country; and thereafter to mind their business at home, and not encumber the streets.

In 1543, under the regency of the Earl of Arran, an Act was passed permitting the scriptures to be read in the vulgar tongue, and the Reformation ideas began to be bruited about. Twelve years later, statues in St. Giles' Church, of the Virgin and certain saints were destroyed; but the then Regent, Mary of Guise, by threatenings, given strength to by her French troops, contrived to keep down open revolt against the old faith. But in 1588, on the festival day of St Giles, the patron saint of Edinburgh, and for which festival the priests and monks had made great preparation, it was discovered that the image of the saint had been taken from the church during the previous night, and thrown into the North Loch. The priests got a smaller statue from the Greyfriars, this the people called in derision "the bairn-saint." The Queen-Regent was in the procession. She must have been a woman of strong character; in her presence all went smoothly, but having left, the populace tore the little St. Giles to pieces, hustling and dispersing the priests.

From the death of the Queen-Regent, and the withdrawal of the French troops in 1560, the Protestant cause was in the ascendancy. An Act was passed denouncing Popery, and sanctioning the hastily compiled Confession of Faith. Penalties on Catholic worship, very similar to those under which Protestants had groaned, and which they had bitterly denounced, were imposed. Any one celebrating mass or being present at its celebration, was to be punished by forfeiture of goods for the first offence, by banishment for the second, and by death for the third. Queen Mary, then in France, and her husband Francis, who held from Mary the crown-matrimonial of Scotland, refused to ratify the Acts, and insulted the messenger of the Parliament.

Next year, 1561, Mary, now a widow, and as such having lost her high position at the French court, returned to Scotland. She waited upon the deck of the vessel which was taking her from the land of her youth, until its shores faded from her tear-dimmed eyes. "Farewell, beloved France," she sobbed, "I shall never behold thee again." When, on the first day of September, she made her public entry into Edinburgh, never had the city shown such an exuberance of warm enthusiasm. The procession included all the foremost citizens, Protestant and Catholic, clad in velvet and satin; twelve citizens supporting the canopy over the triumphal car, where, like an Helen in her matchless loveliness, sat the young Queen. When on the following Sunday she attended mass at Holyrood, her Catholic servants were insulted, and the crowd could hardly be restrained from interrupting the service. And so began the hurley-burley, through six years little other than a civil war; a time of confusion, of plotting and counter-plotting, of intolerance, of malice and revenge; that fair figure with the dove's eyes, but also with a determined will and an unswerving purpose, ever emerging into the foreground, now an object of admiration, and then for denunciation, but always for the highest interest and the profoundest pity.

After Mary's enforced abdication in Lochleven Castle, on 29th July, 1567, her year-old son

James was proclaimed King. The Earl of Morton, head of the powerful Douglas family, taking, in the child's name, the usual coronation oaths. Mary's half-brother, the Earl of Murray, became Regent. Three years later Murray, whilst riding in State through Linlithgow, was shot dead in revenge for a private injury. Then followed two years of discord and confusion from rival factions; and then, 1572, Morton became Regent, and was the master-power in the kingdom. For eight years he was the controlling influence. He was haughty and revengeful, and at the same time avaricious and corrupt; so he made many enemies, and these plotted his destruction. One day when the King, now fourteen years of age, was sitting in Council, one of James's favourites entered the chamber abruptly, fell on his knees before the King, and accused Morton of having been concerned in the murder of the King's father, Lord Darnley. Morton replied that instead of having been in the plot, he had himself been most active in dragging to light and punishing the conspirators. He now demanded a fair trial; but fair trials were not then general. Morton's servants were put to the torture to extort damnatory evidence, and several known enemies were on the jury; so he was found guilty of having been "art and part" in Darnley's murder. To the last he denied having advised or aided in the foul deed; but it is probable that he knew

THE SCOTTISH MAIDEN.

that it was in purpose. He suffered death by decapitation at Edinburgh, in June, 1581, the instrument of death being a rough form of guillotine, called the *Maiden*, which, it is said, he introduced into Scotland from Yorkshire. The gruesome machine is now in the Edinburgh Antiquarian Museum.

In 1596, James, now thirty years of age, quarrelled with his capital. There was in all the Stuart kings a strong strain of the old faith in what hearts they had; or, there was at least a very strong dislike of the independent, self-assertive idea which was the basis of the Presbyterian Church. James granted certain favours, which we should now think simply common rights, to his Catholic nobles, and this roused the ire of the Kirk, then ever ready to testify against popery, to assert for itself the right of free judgment in religious matters, but practically to deny this right to others. A standing *Council of the Church* was formed out of Edinburgh and provincial Presbyteries; inflammatory sermons were preached, and the King, refusing to receive a petition demanding that the laws against papacy be stringently enforced, was mobbed, and seditious cries were raised.

James hastily removed the Court to Linlithgow, ordering the courts of law to follow him there; and he ordered the magistrates to seize and imprison the Council of Ministers as promoters of sedition. The magistrates, anxious to regain the

King's favour, were preparing to obey him when the ministers fled to Newcastle. The King's unwonted promptitude and decision, seem to have borne down all opposition. On the 1st of

JAMES THE SIXTH OF SCOTLAND AND FIRST OF ENGLAND.

January, 1596-7, he re-entered Edinburgh between a double file of guards, chiefly from the wild Highland and border clans, which lined the streets. The magistrates on their knees submitted to him in most abject terms, and many of the nobles pleaded for pardon. James was not a large-minded man,—the more humble they, the more inexorable he. He gave three of his lords charge of the city, declaring that it had forfeited all its corporate privileges, was liable to all the penalties of treason, and deserved to be razed to the ground. We learn that Elizabeth interceded for the penitent city, which, deprived of its magistrates, deserted by its ministers, and proscribed by the King, was in the lowest depth of despondency. James relented so far as to absolve the city on the payment of a fine of 20,000 marks, and the forfeiture to the crown of the houses of the recreant ministers.

Elizabeth died in March 1603, and James was at once proclaimed King of England, and warmly invited to take up his residence in London. On the Sunday previous to his departure he was present at the service in St. Giles' Church. At the close of the service he rose and addressed the congregation in a speech full of kindly expressions, declaring his abiding affection and regard for his native land; and the sighs and tears of the people shewed how their hearts were moved by his words.

Fifteen years later, James was again in Edin-

OLD EDINBURGH.

burgh. His progress from Berwick was one continued ovation. In every town which he passed through, flattering panegyrics, in Latin or Greek, were addressed to him. As he entered Edinburgh by the West Port, he was met by the magistrates in their robes, and the town-clerk read a long address replete with compliments, so inflated and exaggerative, that the dedication to "the most high and mighty Prince James," of the authorised translation of the Bible, reads comparatively flat and commonplace. Afterwards, the king was sumptuously entertained, and presented with 10,000 marks in a silver basin.

Just at this time, the invention of logarithms, by a Scotch laird, John Napier of Merchiston, near Edinburgh, was becoming known in the then comparatively restricted scientific world. Logarithms are prepared tables of numbers, by which complex problems in trigonometry, and the tedious extraction of roots, can be performed by the simpler rules of arithmetic. To the well-educated, they save much time and labour; in the art of navigation, they enable the mariner who may be unskilled in mathematics, to work out the most intricate calculations. In all vessels on the open seas, when observations can be taken, in all mathematical schools and astronomical observatories, logarithms are in daily use. As with other things, familiarity discounts our wonder at their aptitude and value; but the estimate by scientists of Napier's invention is, that it ranks amongst British contributions to science, second only to Newton's *Principia*. Kepler regarded Napier as one of the greatest men of his age; and in the roll of those who were foremost in establishing real science in Europe, his is the only name which can be placed alongside the names of Copernicus, Tycho Brahe, Kepler, and Galileo.

The long sloping street called the Canongate, which reaches down from the centre of the Old Town to Holyrood, was, with its tributary lanes and closes, created a Burgh of Regality by King David the First. It was outside the walls of Edinburgh, and had its own Council of Bailies, Deacons of Trades, and Burgesses. The Canongate is full of old memories. There is the house of John Knox, the sturdy Reformer and typical presbyterian. There is the Tolbooth—the Heart of Midlothian. From the balcony of that old mansion, called Moray House, a gay party were, in 1630, with malicious and triumphant eyes,

THE CANONGATE TOLBOOTH.

looking down upon a crowd through which was slowly wending a low cart, in which was ignominiously bound down that spent thunderbolt of war, Montrose—he is on his way to execution. Aye, but in after years two in that jubilant party—Argyles, father and son—will both also pass up that street amidst jeering crowds, and to similar fates.

Edinburgh Castle is the central feature of the city. Its site is on the summit of a huge isolated rock of eruptive basalt,—rising on the north side,—out of the valley, now a garden, which divides the new from the old town, to about 175 feet of perpendicular height. The castle, with the slopes, occupies fully six acres of ground, and includes barrack accommodation for 2,000 men; the armoury is calculated to contain 30,000 stands of arms. On the Argyle bastion there is a huge piece of old artillery called Mons Meg; it is constructed of wrought iron, and had burst at the muzzle at its last discharge. Its liner is formed of longitudinal bars,—these are strongly hooped; it is thus allied in construction to that of present ordnance, and, rude as the work is, it shows the comparative high state of iron manufacture amongst the Dutch several centuries ago.

The castle was used by Malcolm Canmore and his saintly queen, Margaret, as a royal residence. The oldest building on the plateau which crowns the rock, is St. Margaret's Chapel, said to have been used by the queen. On two sides of the quadrangle called Palace Yard are an ancient hall which has just been restored, and a suite of residential apartments. In a small turret-chamber, Mary's son, James, was born. In a well-protected room adjoining, the regalia of Scotland—crown, sceptre, sword of state, and other insignia—are shewn.

The ancient regalia were "*conveyed*, the wise it call," out of Scotland by Edward I. Robert Bruce was *crowned* at Scone with only a makeshift crown; but it also fell into the hands of the English. The present crown is, from the style of its workmanship, supposed to have been made in the later years of Bruce's reign. It was first used in the coronation of David II., in 1329. Later sovereigns added to the ornamentation. The sword of state was presented to James V. by Pope Julius II. There are also certain jewels which were restored to Scotland at the death of Cardinal York, the last of the Stuarts.

When Cromwell invaded Scotland, the regalia were, for security, taken by the Earl Marischal to his own strong castle of Dunottar, in Kincardineshire. When this castle was besieged by General Monk, the regalia—known to be there by the English—were, by a feminine stratagem, carried out by Mrs. Grainger, the wife of the minister of the neighbouring church of Kinneff. The minister buried them in the church, and there they remained until the Restoration.

At the Union, in 1707, the Scottish Estates passed a resolution that the regalia were never to be removed from Scotland. A hundred years after the whereabouts was unknown,—their very existence a matter of doubt. The following extract is from the article "Edinburgh," in the "Edinburgh Encyclopedia," edited by Sir David Brewster, published about 1815 :—

"At the time of the Union, the Scottish regalia were, with much solemnity, deposited in a strong iron-barred room, entered from a narrow staircase; but most probably prudential reasons have long ago led to their destruction or removal. They were too dangerous insignias of royalty to lie within the reach of the disaffected during the rebellions of the last century. Towards its close, however, some doubts were raised, and a warrant to search was issued to certain official persons. Nothing was found but an old locked chest covered with dust, and the deputation *did not think that they were authorized to break this open.* So the search was abandoned, and an opportunity, *not likely to recur*, of ascertaining whether the regalia were really in existence, was lost."

The *italics* are ours. In 1818, the regalia were found in a search ordered by George IV.—then Prince Regent—in that same old chest, which is still in evidence at the back of the jewel room.

Holyrood Palace, founded by David I., in 1158, was originally an abbey of St. Augustine canons. The ruins of the church evidence the grandeur of the ancient structure. Of a later date is the north-west wing of the palace,—a portion of which was a royal residence of successive sovereigns. One of the complaints against James III. was that he here preferred the society of poets and musicians, to that of the ruder nobility. James IV. was also partial to artists and literary men. In his *Marmion*, Sir Walter Scott has the quatrain:—

SEAL OF HOLYROOD ABBEY.

K

> "Still is thy name in high account
> And still thy verse has charms,—
> Sir David Lindsay of the Mount,
> Lord Lion King-at-arms!"

Sir David was in the first half of the sixteenth century the leading poet in Scotland. When a boy he was page of honour to the infant king, James V.,—carrying him on his back,—his playmate, and, in a sense, his tutor. Sir David addresses the king, giving some early reminiscences :—

> "And the first words that thou gan'st mute
> Were, 'pay Da Lin;' upon the lute
> Then played I twenty springs and three,—
> With whilk richt pleasurt thou would be."

The suite of apartments occupied by Queen Mary are still left, with a portion of the old furniture and hangings. As we wander through the rooms, we can, in fancy, see Mary in the audience chamber, in one of her distressing interviews with the leaders of the Reformation,— when most unjustifiable demands were made on her that, against conscience and conviction, she should renounce the faith in which she had been nurtured,—should change her religion to accommodate the popular change. Or, in the private supper-room, see her and her ladies at their

needlework; or hear one of these ladies sing an old Scots ballad of loves gone astray, and with a sad ending. Then Rizzio's rich baritone rises in an Italian strain; and then there is on these stairs the trampling of armed men, and foul murder is done before the eyes of a queen and an expectant mother; and her life is never the same again.

Little more than this wing of the palace was left by a fire, in 1560, when Cromwell's soldiers were quartered in the building. All the newer portion was built in the reign of Charles II. The picture gallery is 150 feet long, and contains portraits (?) of 106 ancient Scottish kings. Here, in the autumn of 1745, Prince Charles Edward held his mimic court. At every general parliamentary election the sixteen representative Scottish peers are chosen in this hall.

James VI. repaired and embellished the church, providing it with an organ, a throne, and twelve stalls for the Knights of the Thistle. The roof fell in in 1768, and the fine eastern window yielded to a violent tempest in 1795. Since then the church—the sepulchre of Scottish kings and queens—has been allowed to become a ruin.

INTERIOR OF HOLYROOD CHURCH, LOOKING EAST.

Offences and their Punishment in the Sixteenth Century.

THE century which included the Reformation, and the long minorities of three sovereigns,—James V., his daughter Mary, and her son, James VI.,—all periods of strife and unsettledness, was for Scotland, governmentally and politically, a turbulent one. The state was often in confusion; but the burghs were little states, acting by their own laws, under properly constituted magistrates.

The oldest records of the Burgh Court of Dundee which have been preserved commence in 1550, and extend to 1568. These, with other old records, have recently been carefully examined, and many portions trancribed, by Mr. Alexander Maxwell, F.S.A.Scot., and they form the ground-work for his two interesting volumes on Old Dundee. With the author's kind permission, we make several extracts, illustrative of the social history of the period, so far as this is brought into view by the matters which came before the Burgh Court. These records may be fairly taken as a sample of the then condition, as respects crime, of the whole of Scotland.

And three things will be in evidence from these records:—

1. That this was really a Court of Justice; patient consideration given, as a rule, to the cases which came before it; and although some of the punishments may seem severe, and others rather ridiculous, yet on the whole the spirit was paternal, corrective, and peace-making. The penalties inflicted were all on the supposition that the offenders had still a sense of shame left, and that to have the good opinion of their fellows was an incentive to well doing.

2. That considering the unsettled condition of the country, there was not an abnormal amount of disorder and crime. Whisky, that curse of Scotland in later years, had not come into use, and there was no excessive ale and wine drinking. Theft was not common.

3. That a main point with the burgh authorities was to get locally rid of their incorrigibles; leaving neighbouring towns and the country districts to take care of themselves.

That ever unruly member, the tongue, gave a good deal of trouble :—

Reche Crag, baker, being warned that his bread was under weight, charged the officer with using false weights to weigh his bread with, for which insult " he is ordainit to come to the church on Sunday next in the time of high mass to there offer a candle of a pound of wax, to ask the officer's forgiveness, and say, That the word was false he said." James Denman, having " blasphemed " a notary, has to ask his forgiveness, and to pay to the master of the Hospital twenty shillings to be given to the poor,—" and gif he be again apprehendit with the like, to be banishit the burgh a year and a day."

John Robertson and his wife had slandered Katrine Butcher. John sung very small in Court,—" revokit his allegance as nocht of veritie, and he knows nocht of Katrine but honour." John's wife appears to have first uttered the slander in "flyting," and she and he were "adjudgit to come instantly to the Mercat Cross, and there ask Katrine's forgiveness upon their knees: and gif the wife be funden by day or nicht blasphemin any man or woman, she will be banishit the burgh."

For "wrangeous mispersoning of Will Gibson's wife, Jonet Crag is ordainit to pass to the Mercat Cross, and on her knees, with the beads about her neck to say 'My tongue leeit,' and pass with the beads about the town." The tolbooth "beads" were derisively hung on the neck of a termagant, whilst she made a promenade through the burgh. Poor husbands had to bear the brunt of their wives' characters. William Rannald, being about to leave the burgh, "the Council decernit that nae testimonial be given to him; but if he labours for ane, that it be made conform to his wife's demerits, and specify wherefore she was banishit this burgh for ever."

Besse Spens is admonished "that gif she be found flyting with ony neighbour, man or wife, and specially agains Jonet Arthe, she shall be put on the cuck-stule, and sit there twenty-four hours." This cuck-stule had just been put up in an open position beside the Market Cross. To be set up to public derision in this chair was the height of ignominy.

Whilst in these comparatively rude times women's tongues often wagged fiercely against each other, men's wranglings would end in blows. Charly Baxter "sall give to Robert Nicholson, for the hurting of him, forty shillings, but as Robert was also to blame, he sall pay the leech [surgeon] himself. And gif ony of them maks ony stroublance till other in time to come, to pay a stane of wax to Our Lady." So long as the old Church held sway, fines were generally in candles for lighting St. Mary's altar.

The stocks now and again come into the record. For "stroublance of Patte Baxter, Jok Galloway is ordainit to come on Sunday next with a candle of a pund of wax, efter to be given to Our Lady licht, and ask the Bailies and Patte's forgiveness. And gif he will nocht do this, to lie the nicht in the stocks, and ask Patte's forgiveness the morn at the Mercat Cross." Nichol Anderson "is decernit to lie twenty-four hours in the stocks, for stroubling of this gude town and wounding of ane stranger, because he has nocht to pay the leech."

When Rob Dawson "stroublit" Wille Pangell, "he is ordainit to pay the leech for his craft of healing Wille's head breaking, and give Wille twelve pence ilk day that the leech may depone that he may nocht gudely lawbour through the hurt." "Henry Justice is ordained to cause cure Margret Leischman's head, broken by him within silence of the nicht." It was an aggravation of an offence that it was committed at night. Allan Sowtar being charged by Besse Spens for the "stroublance of her and her house, under silence of the nicht, he is amerciate [punished by fine] for the trouble done to this gude town, an if he be founden committing sic fault again, nicht-walking and making trouble, that he be banishit."

The sentences on a brawl in the churchyard, in September, 1554, are notable as being the last in

THE STOCKS, FROM THE CANONGATE TOLBOOTH.
(Now in the Scottish Antiquarian Museum.)

the record where the fines were in the shape of offerings on the high altar of St. Mary's Church. Fines where they were not given as a *solatium* to the injured persons, were generally applied to aid "puir folks." And punishments were as a rule inflicted summarily; lengthy imprisonments, taking the persons away from their ordinary occupations and maintaining them by the labours of others, are quite a modern invention.

The vehemence of an outrageous fisherman is quenched in his own element. "George Blak, boatman, is discernit to be doukit owr the head in the sea, and also to pay forty shillings to the common gude for that he keist Fothringham, ane workman, our the shore [pier], and also struck Andro Cowtie, ane other of them, upon the face." A worthless fellow is awarded the punishment of a woman: "Sande Hay, for troublance made upon Andro Watson, is discernit for his demerits to be put in the cuck-stule, there to remain until four hours efter noon."

This is how an objectionable couple is got rid of: "Alexr Clerke and Elesabeth Stevenson,* being banishit this burgh for their demerits, pykerie, and reset, and grite sumptuous spending by nicht, has contemptuously come to the town, contrair to the statutes; whairfore they are adjudgit—Sande to be nailit to the tron by the ear, and Elesabeth brunt upon the check, and they be again banishit for all the days of their life.

* As a rule—and indeed the custom has not yet entirely ceased in the country districts of Scotland—wives retained their full maiden names after marriage, and in both sexes the christian or given name was held to be—as doubtless it virtually is—the proper designation of a person,—the surname indicating the family or clan to which he or she belonged. On Scottish tombstones to this day, the inscription for the loss of a child by a married couple will read as "Son of John Smith and Barbara Allen."

And gif ever they be fund within this burgh, or ony of them, to be put to deith."

Nice distinctions were made in the comparative guilt of accomplices: Watte Firsell and Duncan Robertson are found guilty of "common pickery of ane puir woman within silence of the nicht," and the sentence is,—"That Duncan sall scurge Watte round about within the bounds of this burgh, as use is; and gif he fails in the extreme punishment of Watte, then Climas sall scurge them baith, in his maist extreme manner. And thereafter Watte to be had to the Cross, and, by open proclamation, banishit this burgh for seven years." Climas was probably the burgh hangman, for the Court assumed powers of life and death. John Wilson has, for diverse reasons, been "warded" within the burgh: "Gif he beis funden passing out of this town, without licence of the Provost or Bailies, to be put to deith without forder proof." In another case the manner of threatened death is specified: "The assize hes convict Agnes Robertson for theftuously committing of pykrie—whilk she could nocht deny, being apprehendit with her—and siclyke, hes convict Jonett Moreis for reset thereof. And thairfore the Bailies ordain Agnes to be banishit this burgh for all the days of her life, and never to be apprehendit within the same, under the pain of drowning. And siclyke Jonett to be banishit for year and day, and gif she be apprehendit within the burgh before the said day, to suffer deith as said is."

Generally in cases of theft, and where there were no aggravating circumstances, justice was satisfied by simple restitution or compensation.

John Cathro is relieved from the charge of carrying away the iron band of Will Cathro's door by his offer to make a new band "as gude as it was at first." John shortly after comes up again "for the wrangous taking of five lilies out of John Gagy's harth, and is ordainit to put in five fresh lillies again." A gleaner who has been helping herself to corn from a farmer's stooks, only has the blanket seized in which she carried it. When there were aggravating circumstances theft was punished by flogging.

"Vehement suspicion," without direct proof, was sometimes held to justify punishment. "James Richardson, tailzour, being accusit of pickrie, is adjudgit to be punishit with twelve straiks with ane double belt, because there could be nae sufficient proof gotten, but vehement suspicion, and syne to be banishit this burgh for year and day." Another tailor is, however, able to prove his honesty. Sande Loke is accused by Jonet Sands, of keeping back some of the cloth that should have gone into her kirtle. The kirtle was produced, and Sande ripped open the seams, and laid it upon "ten quarters of new claith of like breid, and it was found to be nocht minished by the craftsman."

The habit of wearing swords, or "whingers," as they are called, was a fertile cause of quarrelling and personal injury. Sometimes offenders were degraded by being for a time prohibited from wearing swords: thus, William Fyf and James Richardson are, after an encounter, "convict for troublance of this burgh by invading ilk other with wapins; William is discernit to pay the barbour whilk heals James' arm, stricken by him with ane whinger; and baith are forbidden to wear whingers for the space of ane year, or to invade other by word or deed in time coming, under the pain of banishing the party whilk sall be found culpable."

John Anderson "is decernit to pay to the common gude, the soum of five pounds for his unlaw in breaking of the acts, by drawing of ane whinger and invading of Archibald Kyd for his bodily harm, publicly in open mercat; and he sall pass to the place where he offendit Archibald, and, upon his knees, desire of him forgiveness. And his whinger is to be taken from him, and put in the cuck-stule." Jonkyn Davidson "hurt and woundit John Jack in his body, with ane whinger, to the effusion of his blude in grite quantitie." The Bailies for amends "decernit that, upon Saturday next Jonkyn sall come to the Mercat Cross in his sark alane, his head discoverit, and, upon his knees, take his whinger by the point and deliver the same to John; and thereafter the officer sall affix it in the place whair the whingers of those are affixit that commit tulzie within the burgh. And Jonkyn sall ask mercy and forgiveness at John, for God's sake, for his crime; and then sall act himself to be true friend to John, and sall never hear nor see his hurt nor skaith, but will, tak part with him in all lawful things; and sal never draw a whinger hereafter, on ony inhabitant, under the pain of banishing this burgh for ever." Furthermore he becomes bound to pay John by instalments the sum of one hundred pounds. On the day named, Jonkyn, at the Market Cross, made the prescribed atonement, "and then John receivit him in favour, embracit him in his arms, and forgave him the crime."

Penalties for Immorality.

It was not only overt crimes which came under the jurisdiction of the magistrates; they also took cognizance of conduct and habits which were considered indecent, or which might lead to breaches of the public peace. Thus the ringing of the ten o'clock bell was the call to a general clearance of the streets and alehouses, a notification that the burgh was entering into "the silence of nicht." It was enacted that "Nae person be fund walking in the nicht season, prevatlie or openlie in the streets or gaits of the burgh, or drinking in ony ale or wine tavern efter ten hours of the nicht, under the pain of forty shillings * for the first fault, and for the next fault to be banishit; and that nàne sell ale or wine to sic persons, under the pain of banishing."

It was also enacted, "Forsameikle as we know it to be the command of God that there sall nocht be ony drunkards among his people, we therefore ordain that gif ony man be apprehended

---

* The comparatively low value of Scots money is always to be taken into account.

in drunkenness, he sall pay for the first fault five merks unforgiven, for the second ten merks, and for the third ten pounds, to be taken up by the deacons and distribute to the puir. And gif he will nocht mend, but continue, then the Bailies sall give him ane sys [assize] of neighbours, and

REPENTANCE-STOOL, FROM OLD GREYFRIARS' CHURCH.

gif he beis convictit, he sall be banishit for year and day, and sall nocht be receivit without his open repentance." Provision is made for inability to pay fines; this is commuted for so many days in "thief's hol," and the same act to proceed upon drunken women.

And again, "That gif ony men or women be

notit as common blasphemers of the holy name of God, the Bailies sall give them ane sys of neighbours; and gif they be convicted of it, they sall be usit samen as drunkards, quhidder they be rich or puir." But a more summary system than that of assize was also adopted. "Quhasover is

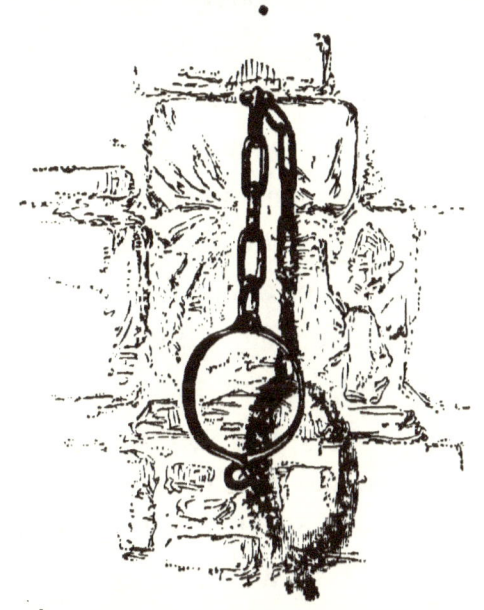

THE JOUGS, AT DUDDINGSTON, NEAR EDINBURGH.

apprehendit banning, execrating, swearing, or blaspheming openly, sall be taen incontinent and put an hour in the choks." This instrument of punishment was furnished with a gag which entered the mouth; and besides the one for public offenders, the citizens were "ordainit" to keep in readiness their own "choks for correcting of the banners and swearers in their awn domestic houses."

It is ordered that keepers of houses of ill-fame, "sall dispatch themselves off the town, or else amend, and leave sic vicious manner of leiving; for gif they be apprehendit therewith in time coming, they sall be openly banishit at the Mercat Croce." Unchaste conduct met with severe reprobation. Men and women were "for the first fault to be admonishit by the preachers to forbear, and to shaw their open repentance publicly in presence of the haill congregation, and so forbear in time coming. But gif he and she be again apprehendit in the same fault, they sall stand three hours in the gyves, and be thrice doukit in the sea, and gif that punishment serves nocht for amendment, they sall be banishit for ever." But the life of a coming child was not to be endangered in punishing an unchaste woman; it was enacted that, under such circumstances, "the woman, of what estate so ever she be, sall be brocht to the Mercat Croce openly, and there her hair sall be cuttit of, and the same nailit upon the cuck-stool, and she make her public repentance in the Kirk."

Exposing offenders to popular derision was a common mode of punishment in Scotland. The stocks and the cuck-stool in the market-place, and the stool-of-repentance in the church, were all used on the supposition that the evildoer had still shame and a wholesome dread of the finger of scorn lingering in the heart. The *jougs*—a hinged iron band for the neck, attached by a chain to the market cross, the gate-post of the parish church, or the tolbooth, atree, or other wise —were a common institution. The offence of the culprit would be placarded in bold characters and very plain terms on his or her breast, or overhead.

ADMINISTRATION OF THE EFFECTS OF PERSONS DYING. DRESS REGULATIONS.

Still drawing upon Mr. Alex. Maxwell's researches amongst the municipal records of Dundee in the middle years of the sixteenth century, we learn that the Town Council, finding that much confusion arose from the improvidence of many of the citizens in not making testamentary dispositions of their effects, it was ordained: "that there sall be twa honest men—responsal, famous and godlie—chosen by the general consent of the haill estates of the town, and power given to them to pass—quhidder they be requyrit or nocht—to visit man or woman in peril of death; and they sall enquire at the sick gif they will mak ane testament, and gif they consent, then the visitors sall despatch and put out of the house all manner of man, and woman, and bairn, except such honest and sober persons as the sick sall desire to be present as witnesses; and the devyse and legacy then made by the sick person to be registrat authentically in the buiks of the visitors, who after the decease of the person testit as said is, sall see the dead's will fulfillit."

The dress worn by burgesses and others was required by law to be suited to the degree of the wearer. In the fifteenth century, Parliament ordained "anent the commons, that nae lauborars nor husbandmen wear on the week day any clothes but gray and quhite, and on haliday licht blue, and green or red; and their wifis corresponding, with curches of their awn making, the stuff nocht to exceed the price of forty pennies the ell. And that nae men within burgh that live by merchandise, unless they be in dignity as Bailie, or gude worthy man of the Council, shall wear claiths of silks, nor costly scarlett gowns, nor furrings; and that they make their wifis and dochters in like manner to dress becomingly, and corresponding to their estate; on their heids short curches, with little hudis, as are usit in England; and as to their gowns, that nae woman wear costly furs, nor have tails of unsuiting length, but on the haliday: and that no woman come to the kirk or market with her face coverit, that she may not be kend." By another act, in 1567, it was ordered "that nae women wear dress abone their estait, except——." The word we omit is spelled in the original the same as that which designates the nymphs in the Mahometan paradise.

Old Aberdeen.

THE following extracts from the Burgh records are interesting, as illustrating the history and the manners of the 15th and 16th centuries.

21st April, 1452.—"The maist parte of the hale communitie of the burgh, consentit that because of perile, the toune sal be stregnthinit with walles, and fortifitt in a gudely manner."

1st February, 1484.—"It is ordainit that the talyeours, and al other craftsmen, sal beyr their taykins of their craft upon their brestis, and their best array on Candilmas Day."

4th July, 1497.—Henry VII. was at this time retaliating on Scotland for the invasion of Northumberland by James IV., and for his assisting the imposter, Perkin Warbeck, in his claims upon the English throne :—"It is ordanit that a watch be set nichtly, for the sayfty of the town against the Inglish, and gif they propose to lande on the northt partis of the havyne, that all mannere of men, with their carts of weir, with horses, gunrye, artailzerie, and all other defensebile wapinnis, be redy, and pass to resist thame, for the saiftie of our Cathedral Kirk, my lord of Aberdenis Palace, our maisteris the chanonis, and ther familiaris and habitaciones."

30th January, 1510.—"It is ordanit that on Candlemas Day, as is the yerlie ryt and custom of the burgh, in the honor of God and the Blissit Virgin Mary, there shall be the processioun of craftsmen, tua and tua togidr, socialie, als honourabily as they can. And in the Offering of the Play, the craftsmen sal furnyss the Pageants; the cordinaris the Messing; wobstaris and walcaris, Symeon; goldsmithis, the thrie Kingis of Cullane; the litstaris, the Emperor; the masons, the thrie Knichtis; the tailyours, Our Lady Sanct Brid, and Sanct Elene; and the skynners the Tua Bischopis; and tua of ilke craft to pass with the pageant that thai furnyss to keip their gear."

4th May, 1511.—Respecting the reception of Margaret, the Queen of James IV., it is ordered that this be "als honorablie as in ony burgh of Scotland, except Edinburgh allanarlie." The poet Dunbar appears to have been present at the reception, and has left a graphic description of the pageant. In the welcoming procession, giving "honorabill salutation," came first the "sweitt Virgin," then the three orient Kings, with their offerings to Christ; and then the "Angill" with flaming sword, driving, for their disobedience, Adam and Eve out of Paradise:—

"And syne the Bruce—that evir was bold in stour
  Thow gart as Roy cum rydand under croun,
 Richt awfull, strang, and large of portratour,
   As nobill, dreidfull, michtie campion:
   The noble Stuarts syne, of great renoun,
 Thow gart upspring, with branches new and greine,
   Sae gloriouslie,—quhilk glaided all the toun:—
 Be blyth and blissfull, burgh of Aberdein.

"Syne come thair four and twentie madinis ying,
   All claid in greine of marvelous bewtie,
 With hair detressit, as threidis of gold did hing,
   With quhit hattis all browderit rycht bravelie
   Playand on timberallis, and syngand rycht sweitlie;
 That seunile sort, in ordour weill besein,
   Did meet the Queen,—her saluand reverentlie;
 Be blyth and blissful, burgh of Aberdein."

26th February, 1512.—"Philip Clerk, bellman," was brought up for passing with his bell through the town, and, on his own notion, announcing that oysters just landed would be sold ten for fourpence, when the boatmen's price was ten for sixpence. "It was ordainit the said belman suld syt dune on his knees, and ask the ownaris of the said oysteris forgiwness: and his crag [neck] be put in the goyf at their wyte."

12th May, 1514.—This was a few months after Flodden, when there was still "a moanin in ilka green loanin," for the flowers of the land "a' wede away" upon that fatal field. "Ordanit be the prouest, consail, and communitee of this burgh, that for resisting of our auld inemeis of Ingland, thar be warnyt nychtly aucht able men, furnyst with wapins, to waicht and keip the town and the cost syde; and that thai haue redy with them fyr and stuf to mak blaise, to warne thar marow's gif thai sal hopin to se ony salis on the cost, likane to wither."

14th August, 1525.—A copy is put in the records of an Act of Parliament just then passed: —"that forasmekle as the dampnable opinzeons of herecy are spred in diuerse contreis be the heretik Luther, and his disciples, it is ordanit that no manner of persone, strengear, nor other that hapyns to arrife with their schippys within ony port of this realme, bring with thame ony bukys or verkys of the said Lutheris, his disciplis, or seruandis, disput or rehers his hereseys or opunzeounes, but gyfe it be to the confusione thairof, vnder the paine of escheting of thair schippis and gudis, and putting of thair personnys in presone."

6th January, 1561.—The Reformation had now made such progress that the churches were being stripped of their old vessels and ornaments. "The said day the town beand lauchtfully warnit to heir and se the silver wark, brasin wark, keippis and ornaments of thair parroche Kirk ropit [*i.e.*, sold by auction], and the same to be sauld and disponit to thame that vill offer maist for the same, and the money gottin for the samyn to be applawdit to the commond weill and necessar advis of this guid toun. And the grytest soome offerit for the same was ane hundredth, fourtie tua pound be Patrik Menzeis for the Keippis,—XXIs. for ilk vnce of silver,—XVIs. for ilk stane of brass, extending in the haill to the soome of fyw hundredth XIIib. money of Scotland." And the articles so sold were delivered to the said Patrik; but not without protest, for, "the said day Gilbert Menzes and Gilbert Collysone dissentit to the said roiping, selling, and disposicioun, for thame selffis and their adherans, lik as thai had discentit and protestit in sic caicis obefoir, as thai alleigit, and tuk act of court tharwpoun."

9th October, 1601.—"The prouest, bailleis, and counsall ordanis the sowme of threttie tua merkis to be gevin to the Kingis servandis presentlie in this burght, quha playes comedies and staige playes, be reasoun thay are recommendit be his majesties speciall letter, and hes played sum of theair comedies in this burght." It has been suggested that Shakespeare was one in this company of London players.

10th March, 1606.—Although Presbyterianism was now the general religious faith in Scotland, certain customs connected with the Old Church appear to have still lingered on. "Intimationne was this day made by the belman throw the haill toune, at command of the prouest and baillies thereof, that no inhabitant eat onie flesche during the time of Lent, nather yet on Wedenisday, Fryday, nor Seterday theirafter, in na time coming; and that na fleschar nor bucheour within this burght presume to sell onie flesche during the tyme of Lent; and that na tavernar nor hostillar within the samen mak onie flesche reddie during the said time of Lentrone; under the panes contenit in his Majestie's actis and proclamationnes maid thiaranent."

26th December, 1606.—Forbes Mackenzie had

his forerunners in these days, and their edicts were of even more stringent application. "Ordaneit, with consent of the haill toune this day convenit, that it sall not be lesum to onie hostilar, tavernar, or vinter of wyne, aill, or beir, to sell or vent onie wyne, aill, or beir, fra ten houris at nicht furth, at the quhilk hour nichtlie the colledge bell sall ring; efter the ringing quhairof, no persone, man or woman, except sic as have necessarie errandis to be fand gangard vpon the streitis or caisayes of the burght; under penaltie efter conviction in ane vnlaw of fyve pundis."

28th November, 1606.—The compulsory enforcement of what were held to be religious obligations was not the outcome of particular forms of faith, or of special times. The Aberdeen magistrates ordain :—" That the haill inhabitants shall repair to the preaching in St. Machars Kirk, on Sunday and Wednesday, under the pains following—viz., the goodman and goodwife of the house contravening, 6s. 8d.; and ilk servant, 2s., Scots."

In the records of the Kirk-Session of Aberdeen, we read :—

"It is thocht expedient that ane baillie with two of the sessioun pass thro the toun every

Sabbath-day, and nott sic as they find absent from the sermones; that for that effect they serche sic houses as they think maist meit; and chiefly that now, during the symmer seasoun, they attend, or caus ane to attend, at the ferrie boat, and nott the names of such as gang to Downie; that they may be punishit, conform to the Act, against brackaris of the Sabbath."

The tendency of the following order would be towards good digestion :—

"It is ordanit that na disputation nir reasonying of the Scriptures be at dennar or supper or oppin table, quhair throw arises gryte contentioun and debate; and that na flyting nor chiding be at time of meit; under the payne of tua s. to the puyr."

Witchcraft in Scotland.

COMMON-SENSE and everyday experience are at constant war with superstition. But superstition dies hard; like a noxious weed which has spread in a fair garden, if plucked up in one place it will appear unexpectedly in another. The Reformers rejected the alleged daily miracle of the Romish mass; in spite of the prayers, the genuflections, and the *Hoc est Corpus* of the priest, the bread and wine still remained bread and wine. They rejected other alleged miracles of the Catholic Church—the healings and other benefits from relics, and pilgrimages, and holy wells. But an influx of belief in witchcraft set in on the ebb-tide of the old faith. Men and women—especially women—were supposed to have entered into league with the spirit of evil; by selling their souls to him, they had conferred upon them in return certain supernatural powers,—generally to the injury of their fellows.

In the latter portion of the sixteenth, and

WITCHCRAFT IN SCOTLAND.

throughout the seventeenth century, a belief in witchcraft was very general in Scotland; and prosecutions for the alleged crime very frequent. That royal pedant, James VI., wrote a treatise against witchcraft. He had himself been the object of witchly machinations. Witches conspired with Satan to raise a tempest and wreck the ship in which, in 1590, he was bringing home his bride, Anne of Denmark. In May, 1591, a Convention sat in Edinburgh, "anent order to be tane with sorcerers and certain practisers against his Majesty's person." An assize was then sitting upon witches, in the business of which the King took an active part. Under torture the wretched creatures made extraordinary confessions,—one was of a meeting which they had with the Devil in North Berwick Church, when, after casting sundry spells upon the King and Queen, they concluded their revels with a dance, the music for which was played by one of the women on a jew's-harp,—and this she repeated at the trial, upon his Majesty's request, for his particular delectation!

As to the punishment on conviction,—about this there could be no dispute. Had not Moses, more than two thousand years previously, written in his law:—"Thou shalt not suffer a witch to live?" No use saying that this law had only reference to circumstances in old Hebrew history, or that the newer teaching was the more enlightened, the more humane, the more generally applicable gospel of Christ. What were now called witches had to die.

Most of those who were thus put to death as witches were poor old women,—often soured and peevish in temper, ready to resent any slight, and to croak out evil wishes and forebodings. And when evils did occur, when sickness came into a house, or blight into its orchard, or the cows' yield of milk was scanty, or the butter would not form in the churn, then the cause was assigned to the spells and cantrips of the "ill-wisher." Often, to raise their own importance, and make themselves feared, these women would pretend to the possession of occult powers,—to the knowledge of potions and charms,—both for the infliction and the recovery of disease; as also of philters to induce love. And they would themselves come to believe in their possession of such powers. And hence on trial, under torture, or after sentence, they would make confession of witchcraft, with strange disordered narratives of

Satanic leagues and unholy revellings. A woman was called a white witch whose specialty was the cure of disease, or the recovery of lost or stolen property; but none the less was she liable—like Rebecca in "Ivanhoe"—to be tried as a sorceress, and suffer the penalty thereof.

It was not alone the old or the poor who were accused of witchcraft. At times young women, and even young men,—and persons in a good social position were so accused. And as an outcome of the crusade against witchcraft, there arose a tribe of "witch-finders." Pretenders to a knowledge of indicative marks and moles and other signs, were permitted to torture the suspects—to extort confession—being then paid their professional fees.

A witch was supposed to have as an accomplice, a familiar spirit,—often in the shape of a black cat,—an incarnation of the Evil one, or of one of his imps. Sometimes the master-fiend held provincial Walpurgis nights, when he assembled all his subjects in a neighbourhood to a high-jinks festival—a scene of wild riot, of blasphemy, and of conspiracy to do evil.

It is to one of these orgies in Auld Alloway Kirk that Burns introduces his bemuddled hero,

Tam o' Shanter. But this poetical phantasy hardly surpasses in absurdity the plain prose of the following indictment against Thomas Leyis, of Aberdeen :—

"Imprimis, upon Hallowein last by past (1596) at twelff houris of even or thairby, thou the said Thomas Leyis, accompaneit with Janett Wischert, Isobel Coker, Isobell Monteithe, and Kathren Mitchell, sorceroris and witches, with ane gryt number of ither witches, cam to the mercat and fish cross of Aberdene, under the conduct and gyding of the dewill—present with you all in company, playing before you on his kynd of instruments. Ye all dansit about baythe the said crosse and the meill mercate ane lang space of tym; in the quhilk dewill's dans, thou, the said Thomas, was foremost and led the ring, and dang [struck] the said Kathren Mitchell, because she spoilt your dans, and ran nocht so fast about as the rest. Testifeit be the said Kathren Mitchell, wha was present at the time aforesaid, dansin with the dewill."

The items of expenses in the burning of Thomas Leys, Janet Wischert, and Isobel Coker, viz. : for peats, tar barrels, coals, and tow,—and to Jon Justice for their execution, as they are to-day found in the Town's Accounts, are a fearful indictment against the enlightenment and humanity of three hundred years ago. But perhaps the last item in the costs of that veritable devil's festival is the most gruesome and repulsive :—

"For trailing Isobell Monteithe through the streets of the town in ane cart, quha hangit herself in prison, and burying of her, 10s."

In that year, 1597, twenty-three women and one man were burned in the university city of Aberdeen for witchcraft.

Holy Wells in Scotland.

A SPRING of water issuing from the hillside, or from clefts in the rocks—leaping and sparkling, as if in joyance at having from the dark womb of the earth come into the light and freedom of open day—has often been the parent of mystery, of myth, and tradition. The knowledge, common in older times, did not enable the people to see that the spring was merely the outflow by natural gravitation of the rainfall on the more or less distant uplands. The licking up of portions of all the strata through which the water had percolated, and which portions, unseen by the eye, but present in the taste, it now held in solution, was thought to be a natural quality of the particular water. And as ordinary medicines are always associated with unpleasantness of taste, so in waters impregnated with mineral ingredients, the harsher the taste, the greater medicinal properties were attached to them. And the higher temperature of many mineral springs was also considered to be an innate property of the mystical, almost miraculous, particular waters. We now know that this is caused by the waters, in following rifts and fissures in the strata, in their passage to their outlet, having had to descend to lower depths, and being thus warmed by the internal heat of the globe: acquiring one additional degree of temperature for about every seventy feet of descent.

As the old Greeks had in their pantheon of the powers of Nature, Naiads—nymphs of the fountain—so in our older folk-lore the streams had their Kelpies or other guardian spirits. When the Christian Church became paramount, the Catholic Canon of saints and angels took the places of the Teutonic and Scandinavian sprites: each spring was dedicated to, or became the property of, a particular saint; and it was he or she who gave the waters their special qualities.

At some of these holy springs or wells it was customary for ailing persons to go, for the cure of their diseases, on the first Sunday in May; they washed in the streams, and left presents to the tutelar saints; pieces of money were put in the waters, or poor people would place needles and pins, or other small articles, therein. On a hill near Stirling was the well of St. Corbet, to which pilgrimages were thus made. To drink its waters was a safe and easy insurance of life throughout the twelve months ensuing. Up to a hundred years ago crowds of persons—including a large proportion of lads and lasses—came to the blessed well, drinking copious draughts of its waters, but too often mixing these with the strong waters of Kilbagie, of Glenlivat, or other such brand. The wise saint evidently did not approve of this adulteration, for with the practice his well lost its life-preserving reputation.

The waters of the well of St. Fillan, in Strathfillan were supposed to be curative of insanity. The patient was roughly thrown into the pool; he was then taken to the adjoining chapel, and left bound therein during the night; if likely to recover he would be found loose in the morning. Mothers brought their weak and ailing children, bathed them in the well, and as a propitiatory fee to the saint, hung a bit of ribbon, or a scrap of coloured cloth, on the witch-elm which shaded his spring.

At Musselburgh was a well celebrated for its healing virtues, and its powers of insuring good luck. Expectant mothers sent their child-bed linen to be sprinkled by the water, and consecrated by the priest of the adjoining chapel, which was dedicated to our Lady of Loretto. Four hundred years ago it was esteemed the most miraculously gifted shrine in Scotland. King James V. is said to have made a pilgrimage to it from Stirling before he went to France to woo his future queen. If the pilgrimage helped to bring Mary of Guise to Scotland—Scotland had little cause for gratitude therefore!

A well at Muthill, near Crieff, was thought to be a cure for whooping-cough; the waters had to be drank before sunrise, or after sunset, through a cow's horn. Another well near by had a reputation as curative of madness. A third well was dedicated to St. Patrick; how it came to be so is not easily understood; for the British Priest who became the apostle and tutelary saint of Ireland, had no connection with the district; and yet his day in the calendar was formerly observed there as a holiday.

In Strathnaven is a small loch of supposed healing waters. There was a rigid rule as to the mode of bathing. Persons must walk backwards into the loch; when at sufficient depth they are to immerse themselves—leave a coin—then, without looking round, walk ashore, and so away.

The well of Spa, near Aberdeen, had a high reputation for its medicinal virtues. Its waters were conveyed from the spring by a long white stone, with the images of six apostles carved upon either side thereof. In 1615, Dr. Wm. Barclay, an eminent physician, published a book on the virtues of this well: giving some extraordinary instances of cures from what seemed mortal ailments, by drinking its waters.

The Reformation brought loss of prestige to the old Romish Saints, and the Scottish Kirk is found testifying against pilgrimages to reputed holy wells. The following is an extract from the Presbytery Book of Strathbogie :—" September 14, 1636. Peter Wat summond to this day for going in pilgrimage to the chapell beyond the water of Spey, compeared and confessed his fault. Ordained to make his repentance, and to paye four markes penaltye. Agnes Jack summoned to this daye for going in pilgrimage to the same chapell, compeared, and confessed that she went to the same chapell with ane deseased woman, but gave her great oath that she used no kynd of superstituous worship. She is ordained to make her publike repentance, and to abstaine from the lyke in time coming."

"Margrat Davidson was adjudget to an unlaw of fyve pounds, for directing her nurs with her bairne to St. Fithak's well, and washin the bairne thairin for the recovery of her health, and for leaving an offering in the well."

Scottish Marriage Customs.

JANUARY and May were considered unlucky months to marry in. In some localities there was a proverb—"A bride in May, is thriftless aye." The day of the week on which the 14th of May fell, was held to be an unlucky wedding day throughout the remainder of the year. Highland marriages took place as a rule in the churches; in the Lowlands the ceremony was generally performed at the residence of the bride's father; but often in later years at the minister's manse. When two marriages were to take place at a church upon the same day, arrangements had to be made that one party should not meet the other going to or returning from church. During a marriage ceremony, great care had to be taken that no dogs passed between bride and bridegroom; and the bridegroom's left shoe had been untied or unbuckled by his best man, to prevent witches casting uncanny spells over the young couple.

The wedding feast was held in the evening,

generally at the house of the bride's father. After supper, dancing began, the bridal pair being in the first reel; from their supposed bashfulness, it was called the *shemit*,—that is, shame-faced reel. Dancing and mirth were kept up until the small hours; but before then the young couple—usually escorted by some of the young folks—had slipped away to their own domicile; the best man and bridesmaid having preceded them, the latter with a cake of short-bread, ready to break over the bride's head on her entering the doorway. The bride was not expected to be seen out about until the couple were "kirkit" on the following Sunday. A newly-made mother's first public appearance was also in church going.

"Penny-weddings," were large gatherings of self-invited guests, each of whom was expected to contribute towards the cost of the festivities; any balance which might be over, to go to help in the new house-keeping.

Prior to the Reformation, a loose practice in the relationship of the sexes, called *hand-fasting*, existed in Scotland. At the statutory fairs, young men and women made mutual selection as partners for a year; at the end of the year, they were free to marry, to live singly, or to enter into other partnerships! It was the duty of the itinerant friars to persuade the handfasts to marry, and by the end of the sixteenth century the Reformers had effectually rooted out the custom. At the Dundee Burgh Court on May 21st 1560, "Compearit John Ray, and oblist him to marry his wife on Sunday next. At the same time James Rollock has become surety that Robert Man sall complete the band of matrimony with Jonet Myln, or else incur the danger conteinit in the acts."

Ceasing to be considered a sacrament, marriage in Scotland came to be looked upon as little other than a civil contract, hardly requiring clerical agency, or religious formalities. A man and woman going before a bailie or sheriff, and declaring themselves husband and wife, constituted a legal although an irregular marriage. And the celebrant—if so he could be called, who was really only a witness to the parties having *married themselves*—need not even be a civil official. Gretna Green had no special privilege in lay-marrying over any other portion of Scotland.

It appears from Burgh records that in the sixteenth century, a women holding property under a trusteeship, was not at any age free in her choice of a husband. Marrying without the consent of her procurators entailed the forfeiture of her property. A mother would retain her daughter's tocher unless she married with the mother's approval.

And apprentices were not allowed to marry without the official permission of their craft. We find from the Dundee Burgh records, that in 1534, David Ogilvy, an apprentice baker, did so marry, and he was expelled from his craft, and "tynt his freedom." But David took the decree fighting! He appealed to the King, James the Fifth, for reinstatement, and the King gave an order, confirmed by the Lords of Council, charging the Provost and Bailies of Dundee to re-admit him to his freedom, and "cause the baxters receive him to their fellowship, notwithstanding that he be marryit within his prenticeship," and decerning that he will suffer sufficient punishment if his term of apprenticeship be prolonged for the space of one month.

A bride was expected—even in such circumstances of life as made her a "tocherless lass"—to have ready against her marriage many articles of domestic economy. In his song "Woo'd and

Married and a',"—written a century and a half ago—Alexander Ross gives a graphic description of a family conference over the ways and means of an "ill-provided" bride :—

"The bride cam' out o' the byre,
   And O as she dichted her cheeks!
Sirs, I'm to be married the night,
   An' have neither blankets nor sheets;
Have neither blankets nor sheets,
   Nor scarce a coverlet too;
The bride that has a' thing to borrow,
   Has e'en richt mickle ado.

Woo'd and married and a',
   Kissed and carried awa'!
And was nae she very well off
   That was woo'd and married and a'?

Out spake the bride's father
   As he cam' in frae the pleugh
O haud your tongue, my dochter,
   And ye'se get gear eneugh;
The stirk that stands i' th' tether,
   And our braw bawsint yade,
Will carry ye hame your corn—
   What would ye be at, ye jade?

Out spake the bride's mither,
   What deil needs a' this pride?
I had nae a plack in my pouch
   That night I was a bride;

"My gown was linsey woolsey,
  And ne'er a sark ava ;
And ye hae ribbons and buskins
  Mae than ane or twa.

Out spake the bride's brither,
  As he cam' in wi' the kye ;
Poor Willie wad ne'er hae ta'en ye
  Had he kent ye as weel as I ;
For ye'r baith proud and saucy,
  And no for a poor man's wife ;
Gin I canna get a better
  I'se ne'er tak ane i' my life.

Out spake the bride's sister,
  As she came in frae the byre ;
O gin I were but married,
  It's a' that I desire ;
But we poor fouk maun live single,
  And do the best we can :
I dinna care what I should want ;
  If I could get a man.

Woo'd and married and a'," etc.

Scotland under Charles the First.

JAMES died in March, 1625, and a few days thereafter his son Charles was proclaimed at the Edinburgh Cross, King of Scotland; but it was eight years later before he visited the land of his fathers, and was crowned as its King in Holyrood. The then finest poet in Scotland was William Drummond of Hawthornden, and to him was confided the address of welcome to Charles. The address was not in verse, but only in prose—run mad! "If nature," it began, "could suffer rocks to move and abandon their natural places, this town—founded on the strength of rocks—had, with her castle, temples, and houses, moved towards you, and besought you to acknowledge her yours; her indwellers, your most humble and affectionate subjects; and to believe how many souls are within her circuits, so many lives are devoted to your sacred person and crown;" and so on. When the subjects' flattery was so obsequious, we can hardly wonder at the amount of royal arrogance and assumption.

The people were a good deal disturbed about the ceremonial of Charles's coronation; an altar was introduced, and some of the rites seemed to savour of popery. He had Laud and some other English bishops in his retinue, and the King soon gave evidence of his intention to carry out the later attempts of his father, to introduce prelacy, with its subordination to the crown, into Scotland. Now the old bishoprics of the Catholic Church had never been formally abolished, but the titles had been held by laymen of mean rank,—whilst the bulk of the emoluments had gone to certain of the nobles. The nominal bishops were nicknamed *Tulchans;* a tulchan being a calf-skin stuffed with straw, which was set up alongside of the mother-cow, to induce her to yield her milk more freely. The bishop had the title, but my lord had the milk. There was thus a framework of episcopacy in Scotland, and James had in the last year of his reign, ordered its re-establishment in full authority; archbishops and bishops to have under himself the headship of the Scottish Church.

Charles now confirmed the division of Scotland into dioceses, that of Edinburgh to include all the country south of the Forth; St. Giles to be the

Cathedral church,—a wall which had been built to partition off the church into two separate places of worship, to be removed. Four years later, in 1637, the King's projects had so far advanced, that a liturgy, moulded on that of the English church—but where it differed, with a stronger flavour of Rome—was ordered to be used in St. Giles's. On the first Sunday of the innovation, the church was crowded; two archbishops, several bishops, lords of the privy council, the judges and city magistrates, being in the congregation. When the dean, in his surplice, began the service, an old woman—Jenny Geddes,—started up and exclaimed,—"You false loon, will you rout your black mass in my lugg?" and threw her stool at the dean's head. This was a signal for a general uproar, in the midst of which the dean had his surplice torn off by excited women. Stones and other missiles were thrown at the bishops: the magistrates called in the Town Guard to drive the malcontents out of the church; but these by breaking the windows, battering at the doors, and wild clamour, drowned the dean's voice, as he again ventured on his ungracious task. In the Greyfriars' church the new liturgy was stopped by popular clamour.

With the obstinancy of his race, Charles persisted in his designs. He issued proclamations denouncing as rebellion all obstruction to his remodelled church, and transferred the seat of government and the courts of law to Linlithgow. These proclamations were replied to by strong protests from nearly every Corporation in the Kingdom, and the *Solemn League and Covenant*,

JENNY GEDDES' STOOL.
(From the Scottish Antiquarian Museum.)

which had in the previous reign been instituted against popery, was enthusiastically renewed, and subscribed by men and women in all grades of society.

Charles sent down the Marquis of Hamilton as his High Commissioner, empowered to treat with the Covenanters. Hamilton took with him to Edinburgh a retinue of nobility and gentry, who were supposed to be friendly to the royal cause. He was met by a great concourse of people, amongst whom were six thousand ministers in their black Geneva gowns. He opened his commission, but the presbyterian leaders would hear of no terms being made, as they said, with Antichrist. So Hamilton went back to London, and reported his non-success to his master. Again he came to Edinburgh, this time with some concessions, the king offering to subscribe to the original form of the Covenant, which contained no mention of prelacy.

Under the King's sanction, a General Assembly met in Glasgow, in November 1638. The royal commissioner protested against certain proceedings, and he formally dissolved and retired from the Assembly: but under its moderator it continued its sittings, condemning the king's liturgy and the imposition of an episcopacy. The reply of Charles was the pouring of two armies into Scotland, one being under his own command. The Covenanters, with whose cause Parliament had identified itself, were not slack in taking up the challenge. They appointed General Leslie, a veteran from the wars of Gustavus Adolphus, to the command of a hastily raised army. He seized on all the fortified places; and he fortified Leith, to defend Edinburgh from the king's fleet. In view of these warlike preparations, Charles temporized, and a vague kind of treaty was negotiated. Another General Assembly met next year in Edinburgh; and here the Royal Commissioner gave formal sanction to the decisions of the Glasgow Assembly. This sanction was received with an outburst of enthusiastic gratitude; and loyalty—never far from a Scotchman's heart—was again in the ascendant. But it was a delusion and a snare. The king repudiated the concessions of his own commissioner, prorogued the Parliament which met to sanction the proceedings of the assembly, and prepared for a fresh invasion of Scotland. The Scots anticipated his purpose by sending their army into England—where many were friendly to their cause. There was a battle at Newburn, on the Tyne, in which the royal troops were defeated. The Scots occupied Newcastle—and negotiations were again opened for peace.

And Charles had by this time embroiled himself with his English subjects. He had tried to raise money by other means than through Parliament. A Parliament sitting in 1628, had refused him supplies for carrying on a war with Spain; it had also challenged his assumed right to imprison his subjects on his own warrant; and they presented to him what was called a *Petition of Right*, claiming exemption from arbitrary taxation and imprisonment. Charles found it expedient for the moment to sanction this Bill; but soon thereafter he dissolved Parliament, and obstinately refused to call another. For eleven years, under the influence and with the aid of Archbishop Laud, and Wentworth, Earl of Stratford, he played at the dangerous game of *Thorough*. He governed as an irresponsible autocrat, arbitrarily levying taxes, and imprisoning obnoxious opponents, in defiance of the Petition of Right. The *Puritans*, or church reformers, suffered severely. Many were dragged before a court, unknown to the constitution or common law, called the Star Chamber, which professed to take cognisance of offences against religion and the royal prerogative. Men of piety, of learning and worth, were imprisoned, were scourged through the streets, had their noses slit, or their ears cropped, for expressing differences of opinion on even minor matters in the policy of the church or the state.

Who were the Puritans? For answer we must go back to the English reign of James. There had been considerable intercourse between the Reformers of the two kingdoms, and the more democratic and anti-Romish constitution of the Scottish Church, had had many sympathisers in England. From these a party was formed, which came to be called Puritans; they were not dissenters,—none such being then recognised in the country; but were chiefly English clergymen. A petition, signed by nearly a thousand clergymen, was presented to the King, praying for a revision of the Book of Common Prayer,—the disuse of the surplice in reading, of the sign of the cross in baptism, and of bowing at the name of Jesus; also for a reform in the distribution of patronage, and the abolition of pluralities. James, in full court, and with a number of church dignitaries present, received the four professors of divinity in the universities, who represented the petitioners. The King prided himself on his polemical powers; he argued dogmatically, browbeat the professors—asserting his superior knowledge of divinity, and declared that uniformity should be enforced under severe pains and penalties. And the lay and ecclesiastical dignitaries present vied with each other in fulsome adulation. One bishop went on his knees, and thanked God for having given them a king with such divine inspiration as the world had not witnessed since Christ! The discomfited Puritans withdrew amidst the jeers and laughter of the servile court.

But through the later years of James's reign, and throughout the whole of his son's reign, puritanism grew, and threatened to either modify or to disintegrate the English Church. A calvinistic divine, George Abbot, was even appointed Archbishop of Canterbury ;* and many holding church livings were virtually nonconformists. A system of doctrines, which denied the divine right of kings to govern as above the law, was hateful to Charles Stuart. And the Queen, Henrietta Maria of France, was a rigid Catholic; she detested the Puritans, and had inherited from her father high notions of absolute rule; and all through Charles's life she goaded him on in the dangerous path which issued in his destruction. And Laud, almost a Catholic in opinion, and as intolerant as any Spanish inquisitor, directed the affairs of the Church;

* Refusing to licence the publication of some especially slavish sermons, on the royal prerogatives, Abbot was suspended from office, and confined to his country-house.

whilst Strafford was scheming for royal despotism, and to undermine the privileges of Parliament. Clergymen preaching absolute obedience were sure of preferment; the more zealous advocates of *Thorough* were made bishops.

An old levy on the maritime towns and counties, to equip vessels for the protection of the coasts in time of war, was, in time of peace, and on the King's sole authority, extended under the name of ship-money to inland counties, and applied—not to the equipment of a fleet, but to the support of a standing army; and, before this army, all constitutional privileges were to be swept away. In 1637, a Buckinghamshire gentleman, John Hampden, refused to pay the guinea-and-a-half levied on his estate; but the Court of Exchequer upheld the tax.

And, hunted and persecuted, dragged before Laud's High Commission on the most paltry charges, and by it subjected to fines, to personal injuries and imprisonment, many Puritans emigrated; some went to Holland, but the greater number to America: and these became a considerable factor in shaping the social, political, and religious history of the Greater Britain beyond the Atlantic. Three men who came to be of special note in our home history—John Hampden, John Pym, and Oliver Cromwell, were on board, bound for New England, when a government order came to stop the sailing of the vessel.

When the Scots were threatening Northumberland, the King was at his wit's end to raise money to pay his troops, and, as a last resource, he summoned a parliament. The objects were declared in the opening speech to be, to put down the Scots by the sword, and to raise money to pay the costs which had already been incurred in the war. To rouse their patriotism, the King read an intercepted letter from the Lords of the Covenant to the French King, asking for assistance, in the name of the old alliance between the two countries. But the appeal fell flat, the English Commons looked upon the Scottish insurgents more as allies than as enemies, and with kindred grievances to be redressed. So they would grant the King no money until they had settled other matters with him; and after eighteen days spent in wrangling, he called them to the bar of the House of Lords, and haughtily dismissed them.

Meanwhile, the Scots holding Newcastle,

commanded the coal supply of London; and they took possession of Durham, Darlington, and Northallerton. Every town in which the Blue Bonnets appeared, received them kindly, and they kept strict discipline, occupying a good deal of their time in psalm singing and hearing

COVENANTERS' FLAG.

sermons. They professed loyalty to the king, declaring that they had come only as humble petitioners to be allowed to retain their Presbyterian Kirk. Against such meek and harmless invaders, Charles could not raise an effective war-cry; he found that his troops were lukewarm in his cause; he was strongly urged to come to terms with them, and he appointed commissioners to arrange a treaty. The Scots were meantime, from a loan raised by the citizens of London, to have £40,000 a month for their maintenance.

And for the second time in this year (1640) Charles was obliged to call a Parliament. It met in November, and—existing for nineteen years—is known in history as the Long Parliament. Its first session was marked by the imprisonment of Laud, and the impeachment of Strafford for treason against the liberties of the people. Strafford defended himself with great ability, and Pym, who conducted the impeachment, fearing his prey would escape him, got the Commons to pass a Bill of Attainder—a measure for the destruction of those for whose real or imputed offences the law had provided no penalties. Under clamour and tumult the Bill was also passed by the peers, and waited only confirmation by the king. Charles hesitated—what conscience he had was pricked at the thought of sacrificing one whose chief fault had been over-zealous loyalty to himself, and helping him in his designs. But a letter from Strafford, asking the king to leave him to his fate, was enough for Charles;

he signed the warrant, and Strafford was, in May 1641, beheaded on Tower Hill. Laud was for four years detained in prison, and was then executed.

THE CIVIL WAR.

In the early part of 1642, matters between the king and Parliament had become so strained, that both sides began to make preparations for war. On January 4th, Charles had in person obtruded into the House of Commons, and made an abortive attempt to arrest six members, who were especially obnoxious to him. This overt act of the king's roused the cry of "privilege," and in Parliamentary circles excited general alarm and resentment. Upon a demand made by Parliament for the command of the army, the king broke off all amicable intercourse, and leaving the capital, raised his standard at Nottingham, having under him an army of ten thousand men.

The Parliament raised a larger, but a less disciplined and less ably officered, army. On October 23rd, at Edgehill, in Warwickshire, for the first time since the overthrow, by Henry of Lancaster, of Richard the Third at Bosworth, in 1485, a battle was fought between Englishmen. The advantage was with the King; and so, generally, was the campaign of the following year, 1643. He defeated a Parliamentary army at Newbury in Berkshire, and his dashing nephew, Prince Rupert, took Bristol by assault; but he failed to take Gloucester, and lost a second battle at Newbury. Meantime, Cromwell was beginning to take a foremost place as a military disciplinarian and strategist—holding the rank of general of cavalry; his will and purpose came to dominate the entire Parliamentary army.

Charles came to Scotland to try to win over the Covenanters to help him against his Parliament. He would almost go the length of renouncing episcopacy, and he ratified the deeds of the Glasgow Assembly. But the Scots were on good terms with the English Parliament, and were even sanguine of extending the presbyterian covenant into England, where an anti-prelatical spirit was, under the now assertive puritanism, rapidly rising.

On the 1st of July, 1643, an assembly of divines from both countries, convoked by Parliament, met in Westminster Abbey. It was composed of men of learning, of zealous piety and strong purpose; but they were also men· of their own time, sharing in its prejudices, its intolerance, and its admixture of dogmatic theology with the politics and the partizanship of the day. The grand truths, that God alone is Lord of the conscience, and that it is as vain to try to fix and arrest opinions as it is to fix the direction of the winds, or to arrest the tides, had not then come to be rooted in the minds of men. For four years the Assembly sat, arguing and discussing all the points in orthodox theology, and the various forms of church government. The fruits of the "great consult," are in the form of documents which are still the recognised standards of presbyterian faith and worship throughout the world. In August, 1647, the Scottish commissioners reported the results to the Edinburgh General Assembly, and these results were received as the basis of uniformity in faith, to be established throughout the three kingdoms.

In England, the principle of Presbyterian church government was endorsed by Parliament, and a General Assembly and provincial synods were nominally appointed. But, on the one hand, the Anglican Church had many influential supporters; it had now been established for over a century, and had struck its roots deeply in the land; its supporters were by their opponents

O

called *Erastians*, from a German doctor Erastus, who had advocated the subjection of the church to the state. On the other hand were the Independents, who stood out against enforced uniformity, and against any established creed or ritual. To allow of unrestrained latitudinarianism in religious opinions, seemed to the rigid presbyterians disloyalty to the faith,—servility to antichrist. Loudly and rancorously did this controversy rage; the more that the principle of uniformity was pressed, the more did independency branch out into protests against this principle, in new sects—each one more self-assertive than its neighbours. The political destinies of England were now under the arbitrament of the sword, and religious dominancy would be with supremacy in arms.

In Scotland in 1644-5, blazed like a terrific meteor, the course of James Graham, Marquis of Montrose. He had been a Covenanter—vehement, as his nature ever was—but through jealousy of Argyle and other nobles, he took the King's side. He raised an army of Irishmen and Highlanders, and at Perth, Aberdeen, and Inverlochy in Argyleshire, he defeated troops superior in numbers and discipline, by the fierceness of his onsets, and rapid strokes of strategy. Pursued by superior forces, he doubled like a hare, meeting and defeating his enemies in detachments, in Nairnshire, at Aldearn in Aberdeenshire, and at Kilsyth near Glasgow, thus achieving six successive victories. At Philiphaugh, near Stirling, he was surprised and defeated by General Leslie. He fled from Scotland, but returning in 1650, he was made prisoner, taken to Edinburgh and hanged. He was able and energetic,—with the genius of a Napoleon for war,—idolised by his men, but cruel and vindictive to his enemies.

Before Philiphaugh, Charles had been defeated at Naseby, and his cause on the field was irretrievably lost. After holding Oxford for a time, he placed himself under the protection of the Scottish Army, which—in the pay of the English Parliament—was at Newark. He was received with respect—and attempts were again made to induce him to subscribe to the Covenant. What the Scots chiefly cared for was the security of their national church; but Charles was wedded to episcopacy, as that form of church government which best accorded with his notions of royal authority; so he diverged from the presbyterians on a point which they considered of vital importance. The English parliament demanded the surrender of Charles, promising his safety and respectful treatment,—expressing indignation at any suspicion of evil designs against him.

And we now come to an event which Scottish historians must ever approach with hesitation and misgivings. The Scots gave up the King, it is said by his own desire; and this just as, after long delays, they were being paid £400,000, the arrears then due of their maintenance money. This has generally been looked upon as an actual sale of the King to his enemies; certainly it was a suspicious circumstance, the simultaneous occurrence of the two transactions. But the one was not made an express condition for the other the money was due under agreement; and the Scots were tired of the King's presence amongst them; he was rather an unmanageable guest— obstinate, unreliable, and bringing them into conflict with the English parliament, and its formidable and now masterful army.

The King was placed in Holdenby Castle, and parliament, in carrying out their promises to the Scots, opened negotiations for restoring his authority, under certain restrictions; and having sent the Scottish army home, they tried to disband the English army. But that army was now master of the situation—it had Cromwell at its head, and retorted upon the parliament with a demand for the dismissal of the presbyterian leaders—and claimed for itself the right of re-modelling the government. Powerless for resistance, the House of Commons had to yield, and the government of England became a military despotism. A Captain Joyce, with a troop of horse, acting under secret orders from Cromwell, seized the King's person, and took him to Hampton Court. From there, on 11th November, 1647, he made his escape; he reached the Isle of Wight, in hopes of being able to cross the Channel; but was obliged to take refuge in Carisbrook Castle; he was not kept a close prisoner, but was allowed to ride and walk about the island.

At the neighbouring town of Newport, the Royalists negotiated a treaty with the Scots, engaging for the King to confirm presbyterianism in Scotland; the Scots to send an army into England to co-operate with the Royalists. In the summer of 1648, a Scottish army under Hamilton entered England, but were defeated by Cromwell at Preston. A strong party in Scotland had repudiated the Newport treaty; the meeting of the Estates had removed from office all who had accepted its engagements. At this time the King and the English Parliament, both confronted by the army, were approaching each other, and Parliament was about to vote that the King's concessions were satisfactory. But Cromwell sent Colonel Pride with his troopers to surround the House of Commons, and prevent the entrance of the Presbyterian members. Some two hundred were thus excluded, and the independent members voted thanks to Cromwell, and gave his after-proceedings the colour of legality. Within eight weeks thereafter, the headsman's axe put an end to Charles's troubles.

Scotland under Cromwell.

A SCOTTISH deputation visited the younger Charles at the Hague. After a good deal of finessing it was agreed that Charles would be accepted as King of Scotland, conditionally,—on the side of the deputation, that he subscribed the Covenant; and on his side, that the Scots should furnish an army to help him in the assertion of his English rights. He signed the Covenant before landing at the mouth of the Spey, in June, 1650. Cromwell again proved himself the man of the hour. He had just stamped out with an iron heel a rebellion in Ireland; and, within a month from the landing of Charles, he and his Irish army had crossed the Tweed, and were marching on Edinburgh.

He had as his opponent the cautious old veteran, General Leslie. Leslie caused the country in the line of Cromwell's march to be laid waste. The Ironsides had to contend with an enemy against which their indomitable charges in the field were of no avail,—famine. Leslie's tactics were to avoid a battle; but he hovered menacingly round Cromwell, maintaining the more favourable positions. The Lord-General saw no way out of his difficulty, but either surrender or a fool-hardy attack on the strong, well-posted Scottish army. Hemmed in on the shore near Dunbar, but in communication with his ships, he was arranging to send off his camp baggage by sea, and then, by a sudden attack with his horse, to cut his way through the Scottish army, when the mis-timed zeal of the Presbyterian preachers solved the difficulty for him. "Go down and smite your enemies," these preachers shouted, and Leslie's safer generalship was borne down by the clamour. On a stormy morning—the 3rd of September, 1650—the Scots descended to the open plains. Cromwell at the sight exclaimed, "The Lord hath delivered them into our hands." The wet and weary Scots, not allowed time to form in proper order of battle, were totally routed; thousands falling in the battle and the flight.

When the news of the defeat reached Edinburgh, the magistrates fled to the headquarters of the Scottish army at Stirling. Four days after the battle, Cromwell took possession of the city, but it was not till the end of December that the castle surrendered. Other fortresses, Glasgow, and all Scotland south of the Forth, submitted to Cromwell. But the Scottish army was so strongly posted at Stirling that he did not attempt to dislodge it. In the western shires, a party calling themselves Remonstrators, opposed to Charles, and also to Cromwell and his army of Independents, raised an army of about four thousand men, and attacked a body of English troops at Hamilton. They were at first successful, but through their very success they got into disorder, and were ultimately defeated.

The Scottish Parliament, having retired beyond the Forth, now ordered that Charles should be crowned at Scone. He was residing in Perth, and had been so preached at, prayed for, and pelted with good advice, that his patience became exhausted, and one day he made a bolt for the highlands. He reached Clova, a village amongst the Grampians, expecting to find there a large concourse of Royalists, pure and simple. But very few such met him, and he returned to Perth with a small party which had been sent after him.

On 1st January, 1651, the coronation took place. A sermon was preached, in which the insincerity of the Stuart family was a leading topic. Then Charles swore to the Covenants, and to the maintenance of the Presbyterian Kirk, and he was duly crowned and annointed King of Scotland. Thereafter, not being lacking in personal courage, he took a more prominent place in the field. He was sadly in want of money. The Edinburgh mint was in the hands of the English; a mint was established in Dundee— then well fortified—but there was a scanty supply for coinage of the precious metals.

The records of the Dundee Town Council give a letter from the king dated from Dunfermline, May 12th, 1651, asking the town to advance by way of a royal loan, one thousand pounds sterling; but the King's personal security was then of doubtful value, and the Estates having passed an Act ordering all the lieges to contribute voluntarily for the necessities of the army, the cautious Dundonians at once entered into such a contribution.

Meanwhile, the northern passes being strictly guarded, Cromwell sent gunboats up the Forth. These were beaten off at Burntisland; but at Queensferry they effected a landing of Commonwealth troops, and Cromwell made his way through Fife, and took Perth. He thus gained a commanding position in the rear of the Scottish army. But his northerly movement left for the Royalists a clear way into England; and Charles expected to find many friends there. So with the Scottish army he entered England by Carlisle; and, by rapid marches, in three weeks from leaving Stirling he reached Worcester. In hot pursuit, to give no time for raising a Royalist army, Cromwell followed the king. He left General Monk with a small army to complete the subjugation of Scotland.

Six days after Charles arrived at Worcester, Cromwell was there, at the head of thirty thousand men. On the 3rd of September—being the anniversary of the battle of Dunbar—a desperate battle was fought on the banks of the Severn, and the inferior Scottish army—for comparatively few English Royalists had joined on the march—was utterly routed. Three thousand Scots were slain in the battle, and ten thousand were made prisoners; the majority of these were barbarously shipped off to the plantations, and sold into slavery. After many adventures and narrow escapes, Charles contrived to reach France. For eight years he was a hanger-on at various continental courts, and looked upon as a hopeless claimant to thrones which had vanished from the earth.

When Cromwell left Scotland, Dundee was almost the only fortified town which held for the king. Many Royalists, with their valuables, had taken refuge therein. In anticipation of an attack by the English gunboats, heavy guns were placed on the river frontage, and other means of defence were hurriedly adopted. A committee of the Estates sat in the town; and when, in the middle of August, General Monk, with four thousand horse and foot, appeared before it and demanded its surrender, this committee issued a defiant proclamation, and then decamped to Alyth, a little town about eighteen miles to the north of Dundee, carrying with them a considerable amount of public money. Monk, by a sudden swoop, captured the committee; some, and amongst them the veteran General Leslie, were killed; the others were sent to the Tower of London, and the troopers enriched themselves by their plunder.

On 1st September, after a fortnight's bombardment, Dundee was taken by assault. Monk had had a training in military savagery under Cromwell in Ireland, and he now beat the record of his master. Not only was the brave governor Lumsden—after quarter had been given him—with eight hundred of the garrison, put to

THE PROTECTOR OLIVER CROMWELL.
(From a painting by Vandyke.)

death in cold blood, but it is said that two hundred women and children shared the same fate. Carlyle, without any note of disapproval, says: "Governor Lumsden would not yield on summons; General Monk stormed him; the town took fire in the business; there was once more a grim scene, of flame and blood, and rage and despair, transacted on this earth." It is said that the plunder of the town exceeded two-and-a-half million pounds, Scots (£125,000 sterling.) There were sixty vessels in the harbour. After the fall of Dundee, Montrose, Aberdeen, and St. Andrews surrendered, and Monk was, for Cromwell, master of Scotland.

And Cromwell was now virtually sovereign of England and Ireland also. After disbanding, with taunts and insults, the Long Parliament,—as a servant of which he had risen to power,—and playing for a little while with a mock parliament, composed of his own adherents, he found himself strong enough to govern without a parliament. At an assembly of notables—1653—General Lambert, in the name of the army and the three kingdoms, asked him to accept the office of Lord Protector of the Commonwealth. With real or assumed reluctance he gave his consent; he took the oath of office, put on his hat, sat down in a chair of state, and Lambert, on his knees, presented to him the great seal. With more ample authority than had ever been possessed by their legitimate monarchs, he governed these islands till his death. This event occurred in 1658, on the 3rd of September, the anniversary of his Dunbar and Worcester victories.

And so this great personality departed. He was only in his sixtieth year, and up to his last year he had appeared strong and healthy. But as Carlyle says,—"Incessant toil, inconceivable labour of head, and heart, and hand; toil, peril, and sorrow manifold, continued for near twenty years now, had done their part; those robust life-energies had been gradually eaten out. Like a tower strong to the eye, but with its foundations undermined, the fall of which on any shock may be sudden." We might add to the above causes for what seemed premature decline, his knowledge that he had a host of bitter and deadly enemies, ever plotting against his life. To live in constant dread of assassination, will eat as a canker into the bravest of hearts.

His character has been diversely estimated, according to the standpoint of the critic. To a strong believer in force of will and energy of purpose, like the writer quoted above, he is England's greatest soldier, statesman, and ruler. Others have called him hypocrite,—dogmatic, vindictive, cruel to ferocity. Of his administrative abilities, his unswerving resolution, and his military genius, there can hardly be two opinions. Under his government there was peace and order, social progress, and comparative freedom at home; abroad, the Commonwealth achieved high honour and respect. As a victorious soldier, Cromwell shewed little magnanimity towards the vanquished. Retaliation and revenge were common faults of the times—say his apologists; yes, but a truly noble character will rise above the sins and shortcomings of his times; he will be the prophet and pioneer of better times.

As to Cromwell's religious professions, they were doubtless sincere, but men make their gods after their own hearts, and his god was the Jehovah of the old Hebrews; a god of war and of vengeance, rather than the All-Merciful Father of the Sermon on the Mount. Macaulay has said of the theologically-flavoured political writings of the Puritans, that one might think their authors had never read the New Testament at all, so full were they of "smiting the Amalekites," of "hewing Agag to pieces," and of the hard and bitter spirit of the older times. Can we wonder that the mind of the Prince of the Puritans had, unconsciously perhaps, run in the same narrow groove?

Of the Scottish rule of "His Highness, the Lord Protector," it may be said that after a long period of conflict and general unsettledness, it was a time of peace. The laws were administered, even amongst highland hills and border wastelands. Monk, with a small army, and a few forts garrisoned by English troops, managed, after their several defeats, to keep a brave, and naturally a patriotic and freedom-loving people, in thorough subjection. They did not love the man; but, although he would not allow the General Assembly to sit, their church had that freedom of worship which under a Covenanted king they had failed to accomplish. There were two leading Presbyterian parties, the *Resolutionists*, who had placed the Scottish crown on the head of Charles, and still called themselves king's men, praying for him in the public devotions; and the *Remonstrators*, who had never, in spite of all his oaths and promises, adopted or believed in Charles, and studiously kept him out of their prayers. (One might have thought that the worse a man he was, the more he needed praying for). Cromwell favoured the latter party, making a certificate from three or four of its ministers the condition of a minister, although he might be called to a church, being paid his stipend. Cromwell taxed the Scots very heavily, but perhaps, all considered, they got fair value for their money. On the whole, so far as Scotland was concerned, we may indorse what, in his *History of his own Time*, Bishop Burnet says of the Protectorate generally :—" There was good justice done, and vice was suppressed and punished. So that we always reckon those eight years of Usurpation a time of great peace and prosperity."

Scotland under Charles the Second.

AT the death of Cromwell there was not, in the general aspect of political matters, any definite forecast of what twelve months after would be the form of government; certainly an easy and unopposed restoration of the Stuart monarchy was about the last idea, warranted by the history of the previous fifteen years. But one man, the still-tongued, close-minded General Monk, solved the question. By his influence as head of the army, and his tact and sagacity in party wire-pulling, he so managed that within eight months of the Protector's death, Charles II. was quietly proclaimed King of Great Britain and Ireland. It was a twenty-seven years of as mean rule, as has ever darkened the pages of British history. Retaliations and persecutions—one long attempt to turn back the stream of progress—a corrupt court, leavening the national life with foulness and frivolity, such might be the general headings of the chapters chronicling the reign of the "Merry Monarch."

The restoration was in England baptized in blood. Ten "regicides" were hanged at Charing Cross. This was harsh—revengeful; but not despicable or unprecedented. But it is with disgust, with shame for our common humanity, that we learn that the bodies of Cromwell, Ireton, and Bradshaw were taken from their graves in Westminster Abbey, and on the death anniversary (30th January) of " King Charles the Martyr," drawn on hurdles to Tyburn, and there hung on the gallows; then the heads cut off and fixed on Westminster Hall.

And Scotland must not be left without examples of severity. The Marquis of Argyle was the first victim. At the coronation of Charles at Scone, he was the noble who placed the crown on the king's head. But Charles hated him as a leader of the presbyterians, who then held him in irksome tutelage. After a most unfair trial, nothing tangible being found against him except some private letters to General Monk, in which he expressed himself favourable to Cromwell, he was found guilty, and condemned to death. He met his fate with great firmness, saying that if he could not brave death like a Roman, he could submit to it like a Christian.

Other victims followed. Swinburne has said of Mary of Scotland, "A kinder or more faithful friend, a deadlier or more dangerous enemy, it would be impossible to dread or to desire." Mary's descendants were noways remarkable for fidelity in friendship, but they were implacable in their hatreds. When he was in the over-careful hands of the Covenanters, Charles had treasured up against a day of vengeance, many affronts, brow-beatings, and intimidations, and now he meant, in his stubborn way, to demand payment, with heavy interest, of the old debts.

And so Charles, the Covenanted King of Scotland, and in whose cause its best blood had been shed, had nothing but hatred for the land of his fathers, and for its presbyterian faith. A packed and subservient Scottish Parliament proceeded to pass, first a Rescissory Act, rescinding all statutes, good and bad, which had been passed since the commencement of the civil wars; and next, an Act of Supremacy, making the king supreme judge in all matters, both civil and ecclesiastical. Charles soon made it evident that he meant to establish episcopacy. James Sharpe, minister of the little Fifeshire town of Crail, was sent to London to look after presbyterian interests; he was got at on the selfish side, and made archbishop of St. Andrews. Nine other pliant Scottish ministers received episcopal ordination in Westminster Abbey.

On the third anniversary of the Restoration, 29th May, 1662, copies of the Covenants were in Edinburgh publicly torn to pieces by the common hangman. The ministers were ordered to attend diocesan meetings, and to acknowledge the authority of their bishops. The majority acquiesced; but it is pleasing to learn that nearly four hundred resigned their livings, rather than submit to the prelatic yoke. To take the places of the *recusants*, a hosts of *curates*, often persons of mean character and culture, were ordained. The people did not like the men thus thrust upon them as ministers, and they still sought the services of their old pastors; hence originated the "conventicles," a contemptuous title for a meeting-place of dissenters.

And now began, chiefly in the west and south of Scotland, those field meetings which afterwards became so notable. At first they were simply assemblies for worship, no arms were worn; after service a quiet dispersal. But, as signifying nonconformity to prescribed forms, they gave great offence. A new Act forbade, under punishment for sedition, any preaching without the sanction of the bishops; and inflicting pains and penalties on all persons absenting themselves from their parish churches. If fines were not paid, soldiers were quartered on the recusants, and their cattle, furniture, and very clothing were sold. It was even accounted seditious to give sustenance to the ejected ministers.

It can be easily asked, why did this Scottish people, with the memory of their past, submit to these things? There was, as in England, a reaction to an extreme of loyalty; there was the satisfaction of finding themselves freed from English domination in its tangible form of Cromwell's troops and garrisons; there was the pleasure of once more seeing a Parliament in Edinburgh, even though it merely registered and gave legal form to the king's decrees. They were told that the advantage of being governed by their own native prince implied as its price the establishment of that prince's form of religious faith. Their own nobles and many of their ministers had conformed; and thus bereft of their natural leaders, there was weakness and division. Despite of all these discouragements, they were often goaded into insurrections; which were cruelly suppressed, and made the excuses for further intolerance, and still harsher persecutions.

The field conventicles continued. In the solitudes of nature, in lonely glens, or on pine-shaded hillsides, with sentinels posted on the heights, arose the solemn psalm, and the preacher's prayer and exhortation. And men now came armed to these gatherings, the women had to be defended, force was to be met by force. To suppress such meetings, troops were sent into the insubordinate districts, under a wild fanatical Royalist, General Dalziel, and had free quarters on the inhabitants. By 1666, a reign of terror was fully inaugurated; Dalziel flared like a baleful meteor over the West of Scotland. In November of this year, without concert or premeditation, an open insurrection broke out. At Dalry, in Ayrshire, four soldiers were grossly maltreating an aged man, and common humanity could not stand by and look on with indifferance or mere sympathy. The people rescued the old man, disarmed the soldiers, and took their officer prisoner to Dumfries. A resolution was suddenly taken to march on Edinburgh. They gathered in a fortnight's march to barely 2000 men, and

SCOTLAND UNDER CHARLES II. 217

wearied and worn out, encamped on a plateau, called Rullion Green, on the Pentland hills, a few miles south of Edinburgh. Here they were attacked by double their numbers under Dalziel, and, after a gallant resistance, considering their inferior arms and discipline, were put to flight. Some fifty were killed on the field, one hundred and thirty were taken prisoners, thirty-four of

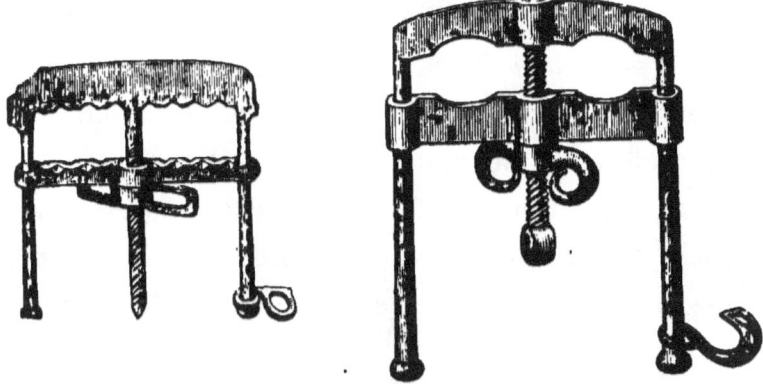

THUMBIKINS.
(From the Scottish Antiquarian Museum.)

whom were, chiefly at the instigation of Archbishop Sharpe, hanged as rebels, and the rest banished.

And tortures—such as have had no place in modern history since the palmy days of the Spanish Inquisition were inflicted to extort confessions of complicity in a rising, which was really the offspring of momentary excitement. *Thumbikins* squeezed the fingers by iron screws.

These tortures were generally borne with heroic patience and resolution. One young minister, Hugh McKail, comely in person, well educated, an enthusiast in his covenanting faith, was subjected to the torture of the *boot*. His leg was crushed, but he uttered no cry, only moving his lips in silent prayer. He had taken very little part in the insurrection, but was condemned to death. On the gallows-ladder his last words were:—"Farewell father, mother, and all my friends in life, farewell earth and all its delights, farewell sun, moon, and stars, welcome death, glory, and eternal life." Seeing what impressions such words made on the listeners, in after executions drums were beaten to drown the voices of the sufferers.

A weary ten years ensued of alternate "indulgence," and renewed intolerance. In 1667, the Duke of Lauderdale was placed at the head of Scottish affairs. He had subscribed to the covenant, and had been a Presbyterian representative at the Westminster Assembly. He was now a subservient courtier, but did not at first assume the role of a persecutor. He disbanded the army, and proclaimed an indemnity to those who had fought at Rullion Green, on their signing a bond of peace. The ministers ousted from their parishes were permitted to return, but on conditions which the strict consciences of many could not accept; and those who did accept were placed under close surveillance, and under severe penalties forbidden to take part in any field meetings. Some of the bishops were good men, striving earnestly to make peace within the church. One of these, Leighton, Bishop of Dunblane, made an attempt to reconcile Presbyterianism with a modified episcopacy. The bishops were merely to sit as chairmen, or moderators, in the diocesan convocations, and to have no veto on the proceedings, but the Covenanters thought this a snare for entrapping them into an acknowledgment of prelacy, and the idea was abandoned.

And Lauderdale who had begun his rule leniently, now afraid of being represented to the King as lukewarm in his service, blossomed out into a cruel persecutor, forcibly suppressing field meetings, and enforcing extreme penalties on nonconformists. It has been estimated that up to this date seventeen thousand persons had suffered in fine, imprisonment, and death. It was said that fines extorted for non-attendance at the parish churches, were applied to supply the extravagance of Lady Lauderdale,—a rapacious, bad, clever woman. Landowners were required under penalties to become bound for their tenants, that they would attend their parish churches, take no part in conventicles, and not relieve outlawed persons.

The gentry generally refused to enter into such bonds; and Lauderdale wrote to the King that the country was in a state of incipient rebellion, and required reduction by force of arms. He treated the whole of the west country as if in open revolt. Not only did he send ordinary troops with field artillery into the devoted districts, but he brought down from the hills a Highland host of 9000 men to live upon, and with every encouragement to plunder and oppress, the poor people. Speaking an unknown tongue, strange in manners and attire, they were to the lowlanders a veritable plague of human locusts. When, after a few months of free quarterage, they went back to their hills, themselves and a number of horses were loaded with booty, as if from the sack of a rich town. But so far as we can learn they were not guilty of personal violence upon those they were sent to despoil; perhaps in this respect hardly coming up to the wishes and expectations of their employers.

In May, 1679, occurred a deed of blood which widened the gulf between the Covenanters and the government, and gave legal colouring to harshness and persecution. In Fifeshire, one Carmichael had become especially obnoxious as a cruel persecutor, and an active commissioner for receiving the fines laid upon the malcontents. On 3rd May, a party of twelve men, chiefly small farmers in the district, with David Hackston of Rathillet and John Balfour of Burley as the leaders, lay in wait for Carmichael, with full purpose to slay him. It appears he had received some warning, and kept out of the way. After waiting long, the band were, in sullen disappointment, preparing to separate, when the carriage of Sharpe, the Archbishop, appeared unexpectedly, conveying him and his daughter home to St. Andrews. To these superstitious men, nursed under persecution by old biblical texts into religious fanaticism, it appeared as if an act of necessary vengeance was here thrust upon them, that instead of an inferior agent, a foremost persecutor, who had hounded to the death many of their brethren, was now delivered into their hands. They took him from his carriage, and there on Magus Muir—suing upon his knees for mercy, his grey hairs, and his daughter's anguished cries, also pleading for his life—they slew him with many sword thrusts.

A general cry of horror and repudiation rang through the land. It was a savage murder; but so had been the deaths of hundreds of persons more innocent than he of offences against justice and common right. More severe measures of repression were taken; new troops were raised, and the officers instructed to act with the utmost rigour. And the Covenanters grew desperate; they assembled in greater numbers, were more fully armed, and more defiant in their language. On 29th May, the anniversary of the Restoration, a mounted party entered the village of Rutherglen, about two miles from Glasgow. They extinguished the festive bonfire, held a service of denunciatory psalms, prayers, and exhortations in the market place, and burned the Acts which had been issued against the Covenant. In quest of the insurgents, and to avenge the affront on the government, a body of cavalry rode out of Glasgow barracks, on the 1st of June. Their leader was a distinguished soldier—a man of courage and gallant bearing, John Graham of Claverhouse—afterwards, for his services in the royal cause, created Viscount Dundee.

In the annals of Scotland there is no name amongst the unworthiest of her sons,—Monteith the betrayer of Wallace, Cardinal Beaton, the ruthless persecutor, Dalziel, with a monomania for murder and oppression,—so utterly detestable as that of the dashing cavalier, Claverhouse. His portrait is that of a haughty, self-centred man; one would think too proud for the meanly savage work he was set to do, but which, with fell intensity, he seemed to revel in doing. In the conflict, he appeared to have a charmed life, and in these superstitious times he was believed to have made a paction with Satan:—for doing the fiend's work he was to have so many years immunity from death: neither lead nor steel could harm him. It was said that his mortal wound, received in the moment of victory at Killiecrankie, was from being shot by a silver bullet.

Claverhouse, in quest of the demonstrators at Rutherglen, came, at Drumclog, about twenty miles south of Glasgow, on the body of insurgents; about fifty horsemen fairly well appointed, as many infantry with fire-arms, and a number armed with pikes, scythes, and pitch-forks. The Covenanters had skilfully posted themselves; a morass and broad ditch in front, the infantry in the centre, a troop of horse on each flank. Claverhouse's call to surrender was answered by the singing of a verse of a warlike psalm. The troops gave a loud cheer, and rode into the morass; they found it impassable and themselves under a steady fire from the Covenanters. Claverhouse sent flanking parties to right and left. These were boldly met before they had time to form after crossing the ditch, and nearly cut to pieces. And then the Covenanters made a sudden rush, and after a desperate defence by Claverhouse, they utterly routed him,—the only battle he ever lost.

This victory of the Covenanters over regular troops, ably commanded, was a general surprise, and it found the victors ill-prepared to follow it up to advantage. They next day occupied Hamilton, and, reinforced by numbers, proceeded to attack Glasgow. They were at first beaten back by Claverhouse, but he thought it advisable to retreat to Edinburgh; and then the insurgents occupied Glasgow. The King meanwhile had sent the Duke of Monmouth—a courteous and courageous gentleman,—albeit the bar sinister ran through his escutcheon—to collect an army to quell the rebellion. On 21st June the Covenanters—who had now their headquarters near Hamilton, on the south-western bank of the Clyde, learned that the Duke, at the head of a powerful army, was advancing towards Bothwell Bridge—crossing which he would be upon them.

In the face of the common enemy, polemical disputes between the different presbyterian parties brought confusion into their councils. The moderate party drew up a supplication to the Duke, describing their many grievances, and asking that they be submitted to a free parliament. The Duke sent a courteous reply, expressing sympathy, and offering to intercede for them with the King,—but they must first lay down their arms. This condition the extreme party would not listen to, and at this most unsuitable moment, they nominated fresh officers —men indisposed to acknowledge any allegiance to the King, or, in matters appertaining to religion, to submit to the civil power. Under Rathillet, Burley and other irreconcilables, 300 men were posted to hold the bridge; they made a stout defence; but it was forced at the point of the bayonet. Bishop Burnet says,—"The main body of the insurgents had not the grace to submit, the courage to fight, nor the sense to run away." But when the cannon began to make havoc in their ranks, and they saw the deadly array of horsemen, and the serried ranks of disciplined infantry preparing to charge—they threw down their arms, and became a mob of fugitives.

And now Claverhouse had to avenge Drumclog. His war-cry on that day had been "No Quarter," and this was his intention at Bothwell Bridge. Four hundred were killed on the field and in the flight, but the strict orders of the Duke were "Give quarter to all who surrender—make prisoners, but spare life;" and thus the relentless swords of Claverhouse and Dalziel were stayed. With the indignation of a true soldier, Monmouth rejected a proposal to burn Hamilton and to devastate the surrounding country; and he issued a proclamation promising pardon to all who made their submission by a certain day.

But the milder spirit of Monmouth found no

place in the treatment of the prisoners taken at Bothwell. They were marched to Edinburgh, suffering much on the way; there, 1200 men were huddled together without shelter in the Greyfriars churchyard—sleeping amongst the tombs upon the bare ground. Several supposed leaders were executed, some escaped further misery by death from exposure, others were set free on signing a declaration never to take arms against the King, and 257 were sent as slaves to Barbadoes.

And meantime Claverhouse was passing as a destroying angel through the western shires. Making little distinction between those who had, and those who had not, taken part in the late insurrection—he seized the property, and imprisoned or put to death, all against whom any charge of contumacy could be laid. The hunted Covenanters were driven into wilder seclusions, and their barbarous treatment naturally made them more aggressive and extravagant in their language. Useless to talk to men frenzied to despair of loyalty to a King, who, in his life of unhallowed pleasure in distant London, heard not, or cared not, for the bitter cry of the people whose rights he had sworn to protect. When they met at midnight in lonely glen or trackless moor, the leaders, Cameron, Cargill, Renwick, and others, would, like the Hebrew Prophets of old, mingle prophecy with denunciation; their high-strung enthusiasm bordered on insanity.

Cameron and Cargill published a declaration denouncing Charles, calling on all true sons of the Covenant to throw off their allegiance, and take up arms against him. And government had now a pretext for putting Scotland under what was really martial law. The common soldiers were authorised to put to death, without any pretence of trial, all who refused to take the prescribed oath, or to answer all interrogations. It was a capital crime to have any intercourse with prescribed persons; and torture was inflicted, even on women, to extort the whereabouts of these persons. At Wigtown, Margaret McLauchlan, a widow of sixty-three years, and Margaret Wilson, a girl of eighteen, were drowned by being bound to stakes within flood-mark.

Amongst many murders perpetrated at this time, that of John Brown, the Ayrshire carrier, stands out conspicuous in horror. He was a quiet, sedate man, leading a blameless life; his only offence was that he did not on Sundays attend the parish church, but either read his bible at home, or, with a few like-minded, met in a quiet place for a little service of praise and prayer. One morning, whilst digging peats for the house fire, he was surrounded by Claverhouse's dragoons, and brought to his own door. Here, his wife and children being by—a baby in its mother's arms—Claverhouse asked him why he did not attend on the King's curate; and John, answering that he had to obey his conscience rather than the King, Claverhouse told him to prepare for death. He said he had long been so prepared. He prayed with fervour, until interrupted by Claverhouse, who saw his wild dragoons beginning to shew tokens of sympathy; Brown kissed his wife and little ones, and he was then shot dead. "What do you think of your bonnie man now?" the devil-hearted slayer asked of the newly-made widow. "I aye thocht muckle o' him, but never sae muckle as I do this day." She laid her infant on the ground, tied up the poor shattered head in her kerchief, composed the limbs, covered the body with a plaid, and then she sat down beside it, and, in heart-rending sobs and tears, gave full course to natural sorrow. The tragedy enacted on Magus Moor was a cruel murder, but if there are degrees of guilt in such an awful crime, that committed at the cottage door in Ayrshire was surely the more heinous and atrocious of the two.

Monmouth remained only a short time in Scotland; Lauderdale was still nominally at the head of affairs. But in November, 1679, the King sent his brother James to Edinburgh, partly to keep him out of sight from the people of England. As a rigid Roman Catholic, standing next in succession to the throne, he was very unpopular. A cry of popish plots had been got up, and an Exclusion Bill would have been carried in Parliament,* but Charles dissolved it, and he never called another; for the last four years of his life he reigned as an absolute monarch.

James, a royal Stuart, residing in long untenanted Holyrood, was made much of by the Scottish nobility and gentry, and to conciliate them he so far unbent his generally sombre and unamiable demeanour. He paid particular attention to the Highland chieftains, and thus laid a foundation for that loyalty to himself and his descendants, so costly to the clansmen. But his

* A concession which was proposed on the King's authority now sounds very strange. It was that at his death James should be King, but for ever banished five hundred miles from his dominions; his daughter, Princess of Orange, to reign as Regent. Parliament would not listen to this rather impracticable project.

presence and his influence in public affairs did no good to the poor Covenanters. Against nonconformity of every shade his only remedies were persecution and suppression. The poor wanderers of the Covenant were hunted as wild beasts. Richard Cameron was slain at Aire Moss. Hackston and Cargill were hanged. It is said that James often amused his leisure hours by witnessing the tortures of the boot and the thumb-screw.

And not the common people only were thus vexed and harassed. Strangely-worded oaths, acknowledging the laws and statutes, and also the King's supremacy, were administered to all holding official positions. When, as a privy counsellor, the oath was tendered to the Earl of Argyle—son of the Marquis who was beheaded at the commencement of the reign—he declared he took it so far as it was consistent with itself, and with the Protestant religion. For adding this qualification, he was tried for, and found guilty of, high treason. He contrived to escape from Edinburgh Castle in the disguise of a page holding up his step-daughter's train. He reached Holland, a sentence of death hanging over him.

And in England, after dismissing the Oxford

parliament, the King was despotic. If he had any religious faith at all, it was towards Catholicism, and thus he took up his brother's quarrel. In the administration of justice, juries were packed, and judges were venal. London was adjudged to have illegally extended its political powers, was fined heavily, and condemned to lose its charters. Breaches of their charters by provincial towns were looked for, and something was generally found sufficient to raise prosecutions upon, the award being always given for the Crown. Fines were levied for the King's private advantage, and by his veto in the election of magistrates he held in his hand Parliamentary elections. The university of Oxford issued a solemn decree, affirming unlimited submission to the Royal authority; and the most detestable of the very few judges whose names are a stain upon the history of English jurisprudence—Jeffreys—was the very incarnation of venality and injustice; he was a vulgar bully, ever finding a demoniacal pleasure in cruelty and wrong-doing.

The country had been sickened of civil war, and public spirit seemed to have deserted the land. Still the Whig leaders of the late majority in

Parliament made some attempts at organizing resistance. Shaftesbury was for immediate rebellion; but Lords Essex, Howard, and William Russell, and Algernon Sidney, more cautiously resolved to wait the course of events, and act when an opportunity arose. They certainly meant an insurrection in London, to be supported by a rising in the West of England, and another in Scotland under the Earl of Argyle.

But a conspiracy in a lower stratum of political influence, called the Ryehouse Plot, which proposed the deaths of the King and his brother, having been divulged to the Government, and certain arrests made, the prisoners, to save themselves, declared that Lords Howard and Russell, and Sidney, Hampden (a grandson of the John Hampden of ship-money fame), and others were implicated. Howard—recreant to the traditions of his name—turned approver. Lord William Russell was tried for treason—nobly supported by his wife—and although the evidence against him was weak, a packed jury convicted him, and he was beheaded at Lincoln's Inn Fields. Sidney was tried by Judge Jeffreys. Howard was the only witness against him, and for a conviction of treason the law required at least two witnesses; but a manuscript treatise on Government had been found amongst Sidney's papers; certain passages on political liberty would nowadays be considered as mere truisms, but Jeffreys ruled that they were equal to two-and-twenty adverse witnesses. He also was found guilty, and was beheaded on Tower Hill. Shaftesbury fled to Holland. Lord Essex—a true nobleman—blaming himself for having put it into Howard's power to injure Lord Russell, committed suicide.

And some Scottish gentlemen were also implicated in the Whig plot. Bailie, of Jerviswood, had been in correspondence with Lord Russell, and was asked to give evidence against him. On his refusal, he was himself tried for treason,—condemned and executed. Many were fined and imprisoned; many left the country, or otherwise could not be found, but were tried in their absence—outlawed, and their estates forfeited.

James returned to London: he feared the influence of the Duke of Monmouth, who, trading on his father's favour and his own handsome face and genial manners, posed as an ultra-Protestant, and, in spite of his illegitimate birth, aspired to the succession. James had Monmouth sent to Holland—then, under the Prince of Orange, the refuge for English and Scottish exiles.

But for Charles the world of time was now at its vanishing point. He was only in his fifty-fifth year when, in the midst of his sensuous pleasures, apoplexy seized him, and Bishop Ken had to tell him his hours were numbered. Certain religious exercises were gone through, and the sacramental elements being brought in, the bishop proposed their administration. The King put this off, and the bishop retired. And now James looked up a Catholic priest, and had him smuggled in by a private door to the King's chamber. The King made confession, and had the last rites of the Church administered. Thus made safe by a Romish passport into heaven— the dying King no doubt enjoyed as a good joke the prayers and admonitions of the Protestant prelates, who, with the lords-in-waiting, were afterwards ushered into his chamber. He died February 6th, 1684-5.

Scotland under James the Second.

WITHIN half-an-hour of his brother's death, James was seated as the King in Council. He declared that he would govern by the laws, and maintain the established church. Loyal addresses from all parts of his dominions were poured in upon him; and the commencement of his reign gave promise of stability and popularity. In a lesser degree he had his brother's vices; but he had shewn considerable aptitude for public business, and was not deficient in personal courage. In 1665, he had, in a war with Holland, taken the command of the Channel fleet. On the 3rd of June a great battle was fought off the Norfolk coast, within sight of Lowestoft. When the fight was at its hottest, the Dutch admiral's ship blew up, and a Dutch fire-ship grappled with and destroyed an English ship. James had twice to shift his flag, as his ships were successively disabled. After an obstinate contest the Dutch ships sailed for the Texel; James pursued for a time,—

eighteen of the enemy's ships being taken or destroyed.

But his accession to the throne was not to be unchallenged. The Duke of Monmouth and the Earl of Argyle met in Holland, and concerted simultaneous insurrections in England and Scotland.

Monmouth landed at Lyme, in Dorsetshire, on 11th June, and marched to Taunton, in Somersetshire, at the head of 5,000 irregularly armed troops. He had married the heiress of Buccleuch, and in other ways became associated with the nobility; stories had been set afloat of a marriage between his father and his Welsh mother, Lucy Walters, and he was looked on by many as the true heir to the throne. At Taunton he was received with acclamations; twenty young ladies presented him with a pocket-bible, a flag, and a naked sword. He had himself proclaimed King. After a good deal of tentative marching through the western counties, he fell back on Bridgewater, and three miles from this town, at Sedgemoor, a battle was fought, in which he was utterly defeated. He himself fled before the close of the fight; and was afterwards captured hiding in a bean-field.

He was taken to London, and at his own solicitation had an interview with the King. A larger-minded man than James would have been moved to generosity, at the sight of his brother's son grovelling on his knees before him, and humbly suing for mercy; but generosity towards fallen enemies was not a distinguishing trait in the Stuart character. And this young man had long been a thorn in James's path; so now no mercy for him—his doom was immediate execution.

And terrible was the vengeance of the King on not only the leaders of the insurrection, but on inferior participants, and on all who had given aid or countenance thereto. There were a number of military executions; and then Jeffreys was let loose upon the western counties. His "bloody assize" was a very devil's carnival of barbarity and death. The campaign was opened at Winchester with the trial of Alice Lisle, the aged widow of one of Cromwell's lieutenants, for affording food and shelter to two of the fugitive insurgents. Jeffreys bullied the jury into a verdict of guilty, and then he sentenced her to be burned alive that same afternoon. Horror-stricken, the clergy of the cathedral obtained a respite for three days. Noble ladies, whom she had befriended in the time of the Commonwealth, solicited her pardon from the King. Her son in the army had served against Monmouth. And James was actually moved to change her sentence from burning alive to beheading! And so it was executed. In this judicial massacre, more than three hundred persons were put to death, and very many who escaped death, suffered mutilation, imprisonment, or exile. Hundreds of the prisoners were presented to the courtiers,—to be sold for ten years as slaves in the West Indies. The twenty young ladies of Taunton, who had figured in the ovation to Monmouth, were assigned to the Queen's maids-of-honour, and they sold pardons to the girls at the rate of a hundred pounds a head!

The accession of James brought no relaxation in the oppressive laws bearing upon Scottish presbyterianism. It was still in the power of the military to apprehend and interrogate, to torture, to confiscate the goods, and even to take the lives of those suspected of nonconformity, or of assisting outlawed persons. It was therefore to be expected that any attempt to throw off the galling yoke would have general sympathy and support. Argyle had himself been the victim of unjust persecution; and yet his invasion of Scotland was as futile and disastrous as that of Monmouth was of England.

Argyle was a Highland chief, influenced by his old family feuds; and his foremost idea was to fight the clans which were the hereditary enemies of his house, and also loyal Jacobites. So with about three hundred men he landed on the western peninsula of Cantyre, and was joined by about a thousand of his Campbell clansmen. He proposed marching to Inverary; but the other leaders were afraid of their little army being shut up in the highlands, and thought that the western shires—in which the covenanters were numerically strong, and where they had already boldly faced the government troops—would be a better field for operations. There was as usual in such differences, much wordy recrimination; time was lost; and when at length a movement was made into Lanarkshire, long, weary marches, with mistakes in the route, disheartened and demoralized the insurgents. The royal troops, in superior numbers, were fast closing in on Argyle, and, without a battle, his following fell to pieces, and himself was made prisoner. He was taken with disgraceful indignities to Edinburgh, and his old, most iniquitous sentence was carried out. Like his father, he met his fate with firmness; he

EXECUTION OF THE EARL OF ARGYLE.

said the grim instrument of death was "a sweet Maiden, whose embrace would waft his soul into heaven." Upwards of twenty of the more considerable of his followers also suffered death.

As shewing the mean and cruel spirit of James,

we may mention that on medals which he had struck, commemorative of his triumphs over Monmouth and Argyle, one side bore two severed heads, and the reverse two headless trunks.

And now in his plenitude of power, James began to shew openly what was his great intention, namely, the subversion of the Protestant faith, and the restitution of papal sway in Britain. His brother had so far paved the way for such a change, that he had taken advantage of the reaction of loyalty at the Restoration, of the general disgust at that detestable imposture, the Titus Oates' "popish plot," and of the discovery of the atrocious Rye House plot, to make his government despotic. He had, by his foul example, sown the seeds of immorality and corruption broadcast through the national life. Religious fervour and high political principle seemed to have vanished from the land,—servile submission to kingly authority was preached by divines, sung by poets, and practised by statesmen,—as the only safeguard against sombre puritanism, political strife, and the misrule of the mob.

And now here was a zealot,—seeing sycophants

all around him; men of position hasting to gain his favour through the Romish confessional; a servile parliament granting him bountiful supplies; and a powerful French king sending him subsidies, —with the property, the liberties, the very lives of his subjects at his disposal,—can we wonder that he thought that his authority could be stretched to lording it also over their consciences?

A century and a half previously, Henry VIII. had abrogated the authority of the Pope in England, and James may have believed that what one despotic king could do, another could undo. Of three things we hardly know which most to wonder at :—the daring of the attempt—or, how nearly he succeeded in his designs—or, that amidst so much apathy, servility, and corruption, he did not, for a time at least, accomplish his ends. But the Reformation was, on the face of it, a natural outcome of a new dawn, after the long night of the dark ages in Europe. It was, with the revival of letters, the new geographical and scientific discoveries, and the general spirit of adventure and research, a stepping-stone towards progress and enlarged political and intellectual freedom; whilst the proposed retrocession to Rome meant going backwards, and a wilful surrender to the old bondage and authority.

James publicly attended the rites of his church; he surrounded himself by Catholic priests, a leading Jesuit, Father Petre, being his political confidant; he entertained at his court—for the first time in England since the days of Queen Mary—a papal nuncio. He placed the Church under the control of a High Commission of seven members, Jeffreys, now Lord Chancellor, at the head. In chartered towns, Catholics were to be eligible to serve as mayors and aldermen. He began the formation of a large standing army, and, in defiance of the Test Act, and in assertion of his dispensing power, he largely officered this army by Catholics. The university of Oxford had, in the previous reign, declared that in no case was resistance to the royal authority justifiable, and it had now to reap the bitter fruits of its servile declaration. The King appointed a Roman Catholic to the deanery of Christ Church; another to the presidency of Magdalen College, and twelve Catholic fellows were appointed in one day. Oxford now began to see that passive obedience might well stop short of a surrender of religious principles; it resisted the royal mandates; and it would not submit, although twenty-five of its fellows were expelled.

And a contagion of conversion broke out in the higher social ranks. Noble lords and ladies of fashion went to mass and confession; processions of Catholic priests were daily met in the streets of London; Catholic chapels and monasteries were becoming numerous, their service bells ringing perpetually.

In Scotland, the Chancellorship was bestowed on one of the King's time-serving converts, Drummond, Earl of Perth. He co-operated with the Earl of Sunderland in England, in driving on James to the most extravagant reactionary measures. By a new court order all persons holding civil offices in Scotland were ordered to resign, and to resume their offices without taking the test oath, ordered in 1681, they taking, for thus breaking the law, a remission of penalties from the Crown; all not obtaining such remission to be subjected to the said penalties. That is,—all officials were ordered to break the law, and were to be subject to penalties for such infringement,—unless by getting the King's pardon they acknowledged his power to abrogate the law! And this test oath had been the contrivance of James himself when in Scotland,—forced upon Presbyterians at the sword's point, and held so sacred that Argyle had been condemned to death for taking it with a slight qualification.

The short reign of James was one of the saddest periods in Scottish history. He had refused to take the usual coronation oath, which included the maintenance of the established church. In spite of this refusal—which impaired the validity of his right to rule—a weakly compliant parliament expressed the loyalty of absolute submission. The law against conventicles was extended to the presence of five persons, besides the family attending domestic worship. If the meeting was held outside the house—even on the door-step—it was to be considered a field-conventicle punishable by death. But on the question of repealing the penal acts against Catholics, Parliament proved refractory, and it was forthwith dissolved.

The King issued a proclamation depriving the burghs of the right of electing their own magistrates. When, to favour RomanCatholicism, he issued his Declaration of Indulgence, by which there was to be general liberty of worship; yet

THE COVENANTERS' MONUMENT IN THE GREYFRIARS' CHURCHYARD, EDINBURGH.

—strange anomaly—the laws against field-preaching continued in full force. Under these laws, James Renwick, a delicate, but enthusiastic field-preacher, was executed in Edinburgh in February, 1688. He was the last in the fearfully long roll of covenanting martyrs.

The Declaration of Indulgence, permitting all professions of religion to worship in their own ways, was published by James—solely on his own authority—in April, 1687. At the first blush we may be inclined to call this general indulgence a step in the right direction,—even although we know that under the cloak of toleration to all forms of faith, the King's main object was to legalise Catholic worship and ritual. We now say, from the more liberal stand-point of the nineteenth century, that the penal laws against the exercise of Catholic rites were tyrannical and unjust. But we have to consider the times in which these laws were introduced, when after a long and bitter struggle the papal yoke had been thrown off,—when the severities of Rome against those she termed heretics were fresh in the memory,—and that she never abates one jot of her assumption to be the one authoritative church —claiming the entire submission of Christendom.

And Dissenters knew that the King was here bidding for their support against the established church. They saw that Tyrconnel, the King's Viceroy in Ireland—a country where James did not require to keep up appearances—was fast arming the Catholics, preparatory to a total subversion of Protestantism; and thus the Presbyterian and other dissenters saw in the Episcopal Church the rallying point of religious freedom; they overlooked its past subserviency to power and its harshness to themselves, in consideration of its present danger, and the stand it was now preparing to make in the common cause.

In April, 1688, the king ordered his Declaration to be read in all the churches. The London clergy met and signed a refusal to comply with the order, and the primate, Sancroft, and six other bishops, presented a petition to the king against being compelled to read a document which assumed the legality of the dispensing power. Only in seven of the London churches, and a few in the country, was the Declaration read. The king was furious, and summoned the bishops before the privy council; on their acknowledging their signatures to the petition, they were committed to the Tower. Their passage down the Thames was a public ovation; from crowded quays, bridges, and barges arose enthusiastic shouts of encouragement; the very officers of the Tower went on their knees for the episcopal blessing. In their imprisonment, the bishops were visited daily by nobles and leading men; and—which irritated James most of all—a deputation of dissenting ministers went and thanked them in the name of their common Protestantism.

And just at this time an event occurred which had a remarkable bearing on the history of the period. On June 10th, 1688, James's queen gave birth to a son. The news had been circulated that a child was expected; the faithful ventured to prophesy a prince; a blessing vouchsafed by the intervention of the Virgin Mary, in response to prayers and pilgrimages. But Protestant England had both feared and doubted. The Court and its household were, almost exclusively, composed of Catholics, and when the birth of a prince was announced, it was generally believed that a strange child had been smuggled into the palace, and was then being passed off as the king's son. There now seems little doubt but that the infant was really the offspring of the king and queen. Thus, to his father's joy, and to Catholic anticipations of the throne being after him still occupied by a king of the old faith—but with general doubts and misgivings—with repudiation instead of welcome, came into the world the ill-fated prince, known in our history as James the Pretender.

On June 20th, the trial of the bishops took place before the Court of King's Bench. They were charged with having "published a false, malicious, and seditious libel." Of the four judges, two were for the petition being a libel, and two were against. The jury had to decide the question, and were locked up during the night. At ten o'clock next morning, when the Court again met, there was a silence of deep suspense before the verdict was pronounced. When the words "not guilty" fell from the foreman's lips, a great cheer arose, which penetrated into the crowded street, and was speedily wafted over London, extending even to the troops on parade at Blackheath. It was a day of general congratulation and rejoicing; and bonfires and illuminations went far into the summer night.

The Revolution of 1688.

BEFORE the birth of the prince, the general idea had been that the country should tide over James's misgovernment as best it could, and wait patiently for the succession to the throne in natural course of Mary, Princess of Orange, the elder daughter of the king by his first marriage. But the situation was now altogether changed; and on the very day of the acquittal of the bishops, there was sent—signed by the bishop of London, several noblemen, and others—an invitation to William to come over with an army to the relief of the country: and the prince at once commenced his preparations.

And meantime, James, his purposes and hopes of success strengthened by the birth of a son, was indignant at his defeat in the trial of the bishops, and, goaded on by the French minister and his inner circle of advisers, he resolved to crush the spirit of the nation by force of arms. He brought over several regiments of Tyrconnel's Irish troops, and their menacing presence, as strangers and Catholics, was hateful to the English people. A derisive doggrel ballad, called from its burden *Lilliburelo*, was sung and whistled all over the land.

And now the king was told that his Dutch son-in-law was making great preparations for invasion. He knew that he had lost the best safeguard of his throne—the confidence and affection of his subjects—and whilst adopting means for defence, he hastened to retract all the measures which had made him unpopular. He threw himself in feigned repentance on the advice of the bishops, and they, in plain words, like the prophets of old, told him of his injustice and oppression, and advised him at once to call a Parliament. He dismissed his priestly adviser Father Petre, and the renegade Lord Sunderland. He restored its fellows to Oxford, and their franchises to the corporations. But the precipitation of fear was so evident in his concessions, that there was no reaction of confidence. The people were watching the weathercocks, and praying for a north-east, or, as it was called "a Protestant" wind.

After waiting some weeks for a favourable wind, and with an after-delay from storms, by the end of October, William was fairly at sea. He first sailed up the North Sea, as if he intended a landing on the Yorkshire coast; but changed his course for the Channel. The wind and tide prevented the royal fleet from attacking him in the Straits of Dover. From the opposite coasts his fleet presented a magnificent sight. There were sixty men-of-war and seven hundred transports, extending twenty miles in length.

It was just a hundred years since such another magnificent spectacle had been seen in the Channel—the Spanish Armada—also bent upon the invasion of England. *Then*, the great fleet meant papal aggression, and priestly domination; *now*, it meant deliverance from this aggression, and freedom of the conscience; *then*, beacon fires on mount and headland flashed danger to the lives and liberties of Englishmen; *now* the tidings that a foreign fleet was skirting the coast were of glad and hopeful assurance.

On the 5th of November—the anniversary of the Gunpowder Plot—the fleet anchored at Torbay, in Devonshire. With his army of fifteen thousand men, William marched to Exeter, where he was enthusiastically received. But the memory of Jeffreys' "bloody assize" was still fresh in the western shires, and for several days there were few signs of encouragement; it is said that he even meditated returning to Holland. But bye-and-bye one nobleman after another, and several officers of James's army, entered the camp. The north of England began to stir in raising and disciplining revolutionary troops, and the Earl of Bath put Plymouth into William's hands.

The King hastened down to Salisbury, resolved to stake his kingdom on the issue of a battle; but William, although a thorough captain in war, wished to avoid bloodshed; he trusted to the increasing stream of desertion from the king rendering a great battle unnecessary. And so it turned out. The sagacious lieutenant-general of the king's army, Lord Churchill, the Dukes of Grafton and Ormond, even the king's younger daughter Anne, with her husband, Prince George of Denmark, and many other persons of note, joined the Prince of Orange.

James went back to London, and sent away the queen and her five-months' old child to France. When he knew of their safety he left London at night, by the river. He threw the great seal into the Thames, and proceeded to Sheerness, where a small vessel was waiting for him. Boarding the vessel he attracted the attention of some Kentish fishermen, who, in hopes of reward, made him prisoner. Released, by an order of the Lords, he returned to London, and passed thence to Rochester. William wanted him out of the country; so facilities were made for his escape, and he was soon at St. Germains, where Louis gave him a friendly reception; and at St. Germains he made his home. Assisted by Louis, he made, next year, an attempt for the recovery of Ireland. In that essentially Catholic country, it seemed at first that he would there be able to retain one of the three kingdoms, but his defeat by William, at the Boyne, compelled his return to France. He died September 16th, 1701, aged 68 years.

The King, having fled, and no parliament sitting, William was advised to claim the kingdom by right of conquest. But both from principle and sound policy he held that this would be a less secure right of possession than would be the choice—as formal as under the circumstances it could be made—of the English people. So he summoned a Convention of the States of the Realm,—irregularly convoked in the emergency, but elected in the usual manner. The Convention

THE REVOLUTION OF 1688.

met on 22nd February—six weeks after the King's flight.

The debates were long and stormy; the two Houses disagreed,—the Lords could hardly bring themselves to declare for the deposition of the King; but the Commons were firm, and at length this resolution was passed in both houses: "That James, having violated the fundamental laws, and withdrawn himself from the kingdom, has broken the original contract between king and people, has abdicated the government, and therefore the throne has become vacant."

And then came the questions,—Who was to reign? and what was to be the order of succession? Here there was a division of opinion. Was James's infant son to be acknowledged as King—with William as Regent? or, Should the crown be conferred on Mary in her own right? William was not a man of many words, but he now got together a few of the leading men, and to them he spoke very plainly: he would not interfere with the right of the Convention to settle its own affairs as it thought best; but for himself he would not accept any regency, nor—much as he loved his wife—would he remain in England as her gentleman-usher. In a few hours his words were all over London, and it was known that he would be King.

So the Convention passed a number of resolutions, embodied in what was termed a Declaration of Rights,—defining the royal prerogative, and the powers of parliament; and the Prince and Princess, having signified their adhesion thereto, it was resolved that William and Mary be jointly King and Queen of England, Ireland, and the dominions belonging thereto; the administration to rest in William. The crown was settled,—first on the survivor of the royal pair,—then on the children of Mary, then on those of her sister Anne, and next on the children of William by any other wife. The son of James and his posterity were thus shut out entirely from the succession.

The Scottish Convention of Estates passed resolutions nearly similar to those in the English Declaration of Rights, closing with a declaration against Prelacy, asserting that there was no higher office in the Church than presbyter.

On the leading question then before the country, their resolution had a more decided tone than that of the English Convention. They declared that James had assumed the throne without taking the oaths prescribed by law, that he had proceeded to subvert the constitution of the country from a limited monarchy to an absolute despotism; that he had employed the powers thus usurped for violating the laws and liberties, and altering the religion of Scotland; for doing these things he had *forfeited* his right to the crown, and the throne had thereby become vacant. The Scottish royalty was conferred on William and Mary, in like terms as that of the English Convention.

BATTLE OF KILLIECRANKIE.

In the crisis of his affairs, James had summoned his Scottish troops to England. Their commander, Lord Douglas, went over to William; but the second in command, John Graham of Claverhouse—now Viscount Dundee—had an interview with the King—assured him of the loyalty of his troops, about 6,500 well disciplined men, advised the King either to hazard a battle, or to fall back with these troops into Scotland. On the King declining both propositions, Lord Dundee took up a position at Watford, about eighteen miles north-west of London, expecting an attack by William. But

Dundee had served his early campaigns under the Prince, having in one engagement rescued him from imminent danger. So the Prince now sent him a message that he had no quarrel with him. Then came James's flight, and the Prince's entry into London; and Dundee seeing he could do nothing more to help James in England, rode back with about twenty-five of his dragoons into Scotland. The Scottish army was placed under General Mackay, one of William's adherents, and he was shortly after sent as commander of the royal forces into Scotland.

Lord Dundee came to Edinburgh, for some time hovering like a hawk over the then sitting Convention. The Duke of Gordon still held the Castle for King James; Dundee had an interview with the Duke and advised "no surrender," he then, with a few horsemen, left the city. (We all know the ringing song in which Sir Walter Scott narrates his departure.) Like a fiery-cross he went through the highlands, rousing the clansman to battle for the fallen Stuart King. The man must have had a dominating personality; in a short time he had assembled an army, feeble in discipline and cohesion no doubt; but, as it proved, good for the kind of work it befell them to do.

THE REVOLUTION OF 1688.

The highlanders were posted on an open slope at the head of the pass of Killiecrankie in the north Perthshire hills. To give them battle, Mackay, on 17th June, 1689, advanced up the pass. When the royal troops entered the defile, no enemy was to be seen,—only the pines towering high upon the cliffs on either hand, and the river Garry rushing swiftly by the narrow pathway through the pass. To the Lowland and Dutch soldiers, who composed the royal army, it was a scene novel and magnificent, but bewildering, awe-inspiring.

Dundee allowed the whole of Mackay's army to emerge from the pass, and even to form in order of battle, before he began the attack. It was an hour before sunset that the highlanders advanced. They fired their muskets only once, and throwing them away, with fierce shouts they rushed down with broadsword and target. Mackay's line was broken by the onset. When it came to disordered ranks, and the clash of hand to hand combats, the superior discipline of the royal troops was of no account. Agility, hardihood, and the confidence of assured victory were on the side of the clansmen. It was soon a rout; but with such a narrow gorge for retreat it became a massacre. Two thousand of Mackay's troops were slain. The highlanders' loss was eight hundred; but amongst these was their gallant leader. Near the end of the battle, Dundee, on horseback, was extending his right arm to the clan Macdonald, as directing their movements, when he was struck by a bullet under the arm-pit, where he was unprotected by his cuirass. With him perished the cause of King James in Scotland. After his death his army melted away, and both highlands and lowlands submitted to the Government of William.

General lenity and toleration were the watch-words of William's policy. The episcopal church was to be maintained in England, and the presbyterian in Scotland; but neither were to ride rough-shod over dissenters. In Scotland, much against the desires of the more rigid, as the Cameronians, there were to be no reprisals for former persecution and oppression. Even obnoxious officials were maintained in their old places. When the Jacobite rising in Ireland was quelled by the surrender of Limerick, a treaty was there made by which Catholics were to be allowed the free exercise of their religion.

William endeavoured to get parliament to ratify this treaty, but two months after it had been entered into, the English Parliament imposed a declaration against Transubstantiation on members of the Irish parliament, and this parliament, entirely composed of Protestants, whilst giving nominal confirmation, really put the Catholics in a worse condition than they were before. The Irish Catholics have since then called Limerick, "the town of the broken treaty."

The Massacre of Glencoe.

TO counteract the spirit of disloyalty which was still lurking amongst the Highland clans, the Earl of Breadalbane, cousin to the Duke of Argyle, was entrusted with £16,000, to be distributed among the various chieftains, conditionally on their making submission to William and Mary. The Earl did not make an impartial distribution of the money; the leading chiefs were bought off, the lesser were intimidated by threats. A branch of the clan MacDonald were settled in a wild valley, Glencoe, in north Argyleshire; a small river, the Coe (the Cona of Ossian—a name which sounds musically sweet— calling up thoughts of serenity and peace,) runs through the valley towards Lochleven—the arm of the sea which separates Argyleshire from Inverness-shire. The valley spreads flatwise to the bases of the surrounding hills, which seem to stand as fortressed walls to guard it from all danger. But in this secluded spot—shut off as it seemed from the outer world—was enacted the basest of all the acts of treachery and barbarity which disgrace this seventeenth century.

MacIan, the chief of the MacDonalds of Glencoe, was an old man, stately, venerable, sagacious. He now charged Breadalbane with having defrauded him of his share of the government money; the earl retorted that MacIan and his tribe had been persistent mauraders over his Campbell clansmen's lands round Glencoe, which was probably true enough, as there had been a feud of long standing between the clans. A proclamation had been issued that—under severe penalties for non-compliance—submission had to be made before the 1st of January, 1692; MacIan, out of a spirit of contrariness, put off taking the oath, and the Secretary of State for Scotland, the Master of Stair, a friend of Breadalbane's, reported officially to the government that the MacDonalds were not making submission, and that they were an incorrigibly lawless tribe of thieves and murderers.

On the 31st of December, MacIan and several of his leading clansmen went to Fort-William, and proffered to take the oath of allegiance before Colonel Hill, the commanding officer. Not being a civil official, the Colonel was not empowered to administer the oath, but, moved by the distress of the old man, who saw the danger to which his obstinacy had exposed his people, he gave him a letter to Sir Colin Campbell, the Sheriff of Argyleshire, requesting him to receive, although after the official date, the submission of the chief. With this letter MacIan hastened on, through snowstorms, by swollen streams, and rugged mountain paths, to Inverary. The road passed near his own home, but he was now in such haste that he went right on; but it was the 6th of January, before he had accomplished the weary fifty miles, and presented himself before the sheriff. The sheriff, considering all the circumstances, administered the oath; he gave MacIan a certificate, and wrote to the Privy Council, detailing the facts, and giving explanatory reasons for his own conduct in the matter.

But the secretary had hoped to have had MacIan in his power, and was chagrined by the submission; so the sheriff's letter was suppressed, and the submission deleted from the records of the council. On the 16th of January, the secretary obtained the king's signature to the following order, addressed to the commander of the forces in Scotland :—" As for MacIan of

Glencoe, and that tribe, if they can be well distinguished from the rest of the Highlanders, it will be proper for the vindication of public justice to extirpate that set of thieves." Burnet says that William did not read the order, but signed it, thinking it was only a detail in ordinary business. Another explanation is, that the fact of MacIan's submission being treacherously withheld from William, he thought that the extirpation meant by the order was, that *as* a "set of thieves" they were to be broken up, and brought under ordinary law. William could not have meant to order or to sanction the horrible event which followed; but still the name of Glencoe ever sounds as a blast of judgment against the fair fame of the Deliverer.

And now, as under the royal order, the secretary gave explicit instructions for the indiscriminate butchery of the whole "damnable race." The passes were to be guarded to prevent any escape. "In the winter," he wrote, "they cannot carry their wives, children, and cattle to the mountains. This is the proper season to maul them, in the long dark nights." A detachment of troops, belonging Argyle's regiment, under Campbell of Glenlyon, were sent into the glen. They were hospitably received, and were quartered amongst the inhabitants. A niece of Glenlyon's was married to a son of MacIan's, and for twelve days there was hunting by day, and feasting, card-playing, and healths-drinking in the long evenings. Glenlyon and a party accepted an invitation to dine with McIan on the 13th of February, but, as had been previously arranged, at four o'clock of the morning of that day, the work of blood began. The old chief was shot in his bed; his wife was stripped naked, and died next day from terror and exposure. The two sons of MacIan were aroused by the musket shots, the shouts of the murderers, and the screams of the victims; they, with many others, men, women, and children, fled, half-naked, in darkness, snow, and storm, into the less savage wilderness. The falling snow proved fatal to several of the fugitives, but it was the salvation of the others, for it prevented the troops, who were to have guarded the passes, from arriving at the time appointed, to intercept and slay all who had escaped from death in the glen. It was mid-day when these troops, by the several passes entered the glen, and they found no MacDonald alive but an old man of eighty, and him they slew.

THE MASSACRE OF GLENCOE.

Every hut was burned, the cattle and horses of the tribe were collected, and driven to the garrison of Fort-William.

Thirty-eight victims: Was Secretary Stair satisfied? Not he; he was mortified that his plans for total destruction had failed. "I regret," he wrote, "that any got away." It is said that two men—one engaged in the contrivance of the massacre, and the other in its execution—Breadalbane and Glenlyon—did feel the stings of conscience, the heart-gnawings of remorse, and were never the same men afterwards.

It was long before the hideous story of Glencoe came to be generally known. On the facts being published, there rose a popular clamour for an inquiry. On the eve of the meeting of the Scottish Parliament, in 1695, it was known to ministers that the war-cry would be "Glencoe." So in haste they got the King to appoint a Commission. After a searching enquiry, the Commission reported that the slaughter at Glencoe was murder; and that of this murder the letters of the Master of Stair were the sole warrant and cause. As a punishment for his great crime, Stair was *dismissed from office!*

The Union of Scotland and England.

JUST at the time when the full realization of the horrors of Glencoe was agitating the public mind, the disastrous Darien scheme was floated. This, the first great national adventure in foreign commerce, was a wild speculation, based upon the fanciful assumptions of one man, William Paterson. His scheme was to establish a trading colony on the narrow isthmus joining North and South America, as a convenient stage between India and Europe. His eloquent tongue, and even more eloquent reservations, produced glowing visions of national and individual wealth. There was a rush for shares in the "Company of Scotland;" for their purchase landowners mortaged their estates, farmers sold their cattle, widows pledged their jointures. Nearly half-a-million sterling was subscribed. Ships and stores were purchased, and in July, 1698, a colonizing expedition of 1200 men left Leith, amidst the wildest popular enthusiasm. It reached its destination, and under the ninth parallel of north latitude a New Edinburgh was founded.

The enterprise was an utter failure; the climate was found to be a deadly one, and famine was imminent; many died, and there was general sickness and debility. Under instructions from the home government, the governors of English West India settlements issued proclamations, denouncing the Scottish colonists as pirates, and interdicting supplies and communications. The Spaniards, claiming the land as theirs, were fitting out hostile armaments. Finding that to remain meant nothing short of extermination, all who were left took to their ships; drifting almost at the mercy of winds and waves, they arrived at the Hudson river. A second expedition of 1300 men landed to find ruins and a solitude, and to meet a similar fate.

Glencoe had largely weakened the popularity of William in Scotland, and his hostile action towards the Darien scheme excited hatred and disloyalty. Jacobitism, instead of wearing itself out, became more deeply rooted and more formidable. The golden link of the crown, which during the seventeenth century had been the only official tie between the two nations, seemed a fragile one;

and the King saw, with the prescience of a statesman, that there must either be closer union, or entire separation. He could see that—comparatively weak as Scotland was—its influence might, under a foreign complication, have to be deducted from the strength of England.

In February, 1702, William met with the accident—a fall from his horse—which resulted in his death. When he knew that his end was approaching he sent his last message under his sign-manual to Parliament, recommending the union of the kingdoms; it would be a comfort to him if Parliament would favourably consider the matter. The Commons agreed to consider the King's message on the 7th of March—on that day he was in *extremis*—dying in the night.

Then Anne, William's sister-in-law, reigned. The Scots were still irritable over the English treatment of the Darien scheme, and their Parliament passed what was called *The Act of Security*. By this act it was ordained that the English successor to the then reigning sovereign, would not be adopted by Scotland, unless there was free trade between the two countries, and the internal affairs of Scotland thoroughly secured from English influence. The Queen's High

Commissioner refused the royal assent to this defiant measure, and the English House of Peers passed a resolution, that a dangerous plot existed in Scotland for the overthrow of the Protestant succession in that nation. The Scots highly resented this resolution, declaring it to be an unauthorised interference with the concerns of an independent kingdom. The Estates refused to grant supplies, and ordered the disciplining, by monthly drills, of all men capable of bearing arms. The reply of the English Parliament was, by the enactment of fresh restrictions upon Scottish trade with England and its colonies, and by ordering the border towns of Newcastle, Berwick, and Carlisle to be fortified and garrisoned.

But the queen had in her minister, Earl Godolphin, a wise and sagacious statesman ; by his advice she gave in 1704, her assent to the Act of Security. And the English Parliament empowered the queen to nominate commissioners to discuss with commissioners appointed by the Scottish estates terms of a treaty of union between the two nations. Thirty commissioners were thus appointed on each side ; ostensibly they represented all parties ; but Godolphin's powerful influence was so exerted in the selection, that not

T

only was there a majority on both sides in favour of union, but also for that union being favourable to England. There is more than mere suspicion that English money was freely given, and English promises of personal advancement were largely made, to induce the Scottish Commissioners to agree to terms which were certainly unjust to Scotland.

The numerical proportion of its population, entitled Scotland to send sixty-six members to a united House of Commons; but the number was restricted to forty-five. Of the Scottish nobility, not one was to be entitled by right of title or of possessions, to sit in the House of Lords; but there were to be sixteen representative peers. For the English bishops holding seats in the upper house, there was to be no Scottish counterpart. The Scottish nobles on the Commission were tempted to agree to the ignominious position their order was to be placed in by the promise that themselves would be created *British peers*, with hereditary seats in the Lords. Scotland was to pay a fair proportion of the general taxation. She was to retain her Presbyterian Church, and her own civil and municipal laws and institutions.

When the articles of the proposed treaty as arranged by the joint Commission were published, there was in Scotland a general outburst of rage and mortification. It seemed as if they were to make a voluntary surrender of their dearly bought independence,—a descent from their position as a free nation, into that of a mere province. When the Scottish Parliament met in October, 1706, the whole country was in a state of dangerous excitement. Addresses against the proposed terms of union were sent from every county and town, from almost every parish in the kingdom. In some towns, copies of the Articles of Union were publicly burned. Edinburgh was in a state of wild tumult; the High Commissioner was hooted; the Provost, who was known to favour the obnoxious treaty, had his house wrecked. In the House of Parliament there were fierce debates, "resembling," said an eye witness, "not a mere strife of tongues, but the clash of arms." The opposition, headed by the Duke of Hamilton, did all they could to hinder the measure; finding their resistance ineffectual, they retired from the parliament house, and, clause by clause, the articles of treaty were formally passed by the compliant majority.

In March, 1707, the English parliament ratified the Treaty of Union, and on the 1st of May ensuing, it came into operation. It had been carried through the Scottish Parliament by transparent venality, and under popular disfavour. It was inaugurated in Scotland with sullen discontent, and for six years it was there the ruling passion to discredit and decry it. And so far its results had not contradicted evil forebodings. As had been feared, the very slender representation of Scotland in the Imperial Parliament, gave it only a weak voice in legislature. The English treason laws, and malt-tax were extended to Scotland. The Scottish representatives in the Commons complained that they were not treated as equals by their fellow-members—not as representing a free nation, the equal of England in its rights and privileges, but a subjugated and dependent province. Sneers at their country, and sarcasms on their own accent, manners, and appearance, were daily met with by men who were proud of their native land, and in that land had been accorded the respect due to gentlemen of birth, breeding, and education. And Scottish noblemen, who had not been elected on the representative sixteen, but had been created *British Peers* by the sovereign, were, by a resolution of the House of Lords, refused seats in that House.

In 1713, the Scottish members in both Houses, —and who included within their ranks men of all political parties—Revolution Whigs, and Tory advocates of kingly prerogative, Jacobites and adherents of the House of Hanover,—unanimously resolved to move in parliament the repeal of the Act of Union, on the grounds that it had failed in the good results which had been anticipated from it. And in the then state of parties in England, there seemed a fair chance of carrying the proposed abrogation. For the Whigs, who had been the dominant party, from the Revolution to 1710, when they were ousted from office, were now—although they had been the active promoters of the Union—prepared to do anything to cripple the government. The defence of the Union now rested with the Tories, who had strenuously opposed it, and obstructed it at every stage.

On the 1st of June, the motion for repeal was brought up in the House of Lords, and after a warm debate was rejected by a majority of only four votes. So, happily for both countries, the

Union had farther trial; and as in the generality of prognostications of evil, as the resultant of political or social change, time has proved their falsity. Under the Union, Scotland advanced in material prosperity, and as a nation she has fully maintained her national prestige. Scotsmen have ever taken an active part—at times a leading part—in imperial affairs. In diplomacy and in war, in science and invention, in literature and art, in philosophy and trading enterprise, Scotsmen have been well in line with men of the other nationalities which together constitute the United Kingdom of Great Britain and Ireland.

The Jacobite Risings of 1715.

QUEEN ANNE was not a woman of strong intellect, but simple and homely in her tastes; weakly obstinate, like the Stuart race. In the earlier years of her reign, with the Whigs in power, she was under the stronger will of Sarah, Duchess of Marlborough; in the later years, when the Tories held office, she was largely ruled by a Mrs. Masham. Her domestic story was a painful one. She passed through a motherhood of nineteen children, nearly all of whom died in infancy, only one son reaching the age of eleven years. Her husband, Prince George of Denmark, was the very embodiment of dulness and stupidity. King James, his father-in-law, said of him, "I have tried George drunk, and I have tried him sober; drunk or sober there is nothing in him." He took no part in public affairs. He died in 1708, and Anne, widowed, childless, and in broken health, was as lonely a woman as any within the three kingdoms which acknowledged her sovereignty.

There is no doubt that after she had lost all her own children, her sympathies were with her father's son, generally known as *The Pretender*. She felt more and more as her life was ebbing to its end, that she had not been a dutiful daughter. In her own loneliness she must have had abiding thoughts of her young brother, expatriated from his father-land. Whilst she was living in royal estate, he, the legitimate heir of that estate, was a homeless waif,—ever tantalized by fruitless hopes and longings. What to her was this second cousin in Hanover,—a foreigner by birth and in all his interests? She was horror-stricken at, and absolutely refused to sanction, a Whig proposal, that Elector George should be invited to visit Britain, and make some acquaintance with the country which he was one day to rule over.

Anne's two leading ministers—Oxford and Bolingbroke, at one in their Jacobite proclivities, were yet at personal variance. At a council meeting, on 27th July, 1714, at which the queen was present, they had a fierce quarrel, and, under the joint influence of Bolingbroke and Mrs. Masham, the Queen dismissed Oxford from office. But the triumph of Bolingbroke was short-lived, for the stormy council meeting so acted on the queen, that she next day fell into a lethargy, from which—with brief intervals of semi-consciousness—she never rallied.

On the 30th of July, when it was known that the queen was sinking, two Whig lords, the Dukes of Somerset and Argyle, took upon themselves, in virtue of their position as privy-councillors, to attend unsummoned the council board. They found the ministers in a state of utter perplexity and alarm; humble enough to agree to a proposal that in the present grave crisis, the queen should be asked to confer the premiership upon the Duke of Shrewsbury. He had taken a leading part in the revolution, been one of William's chief secretaries of state, and was much respected by both parties. The dying queen gave, by a sign, her consent to his receiving the staff of office. That feeble sign was the last public action of the Stuart dynasty. Anne died on the 1st of August, and next day the Elector of Hanover,—through his mother and grandmother, a great grandson of James I.,—was, as George the First, proclaimed king in London.

The new king, knowing that the Whigs were his best friends, formed his ministry from their ranks. Three of Anne's ministers, Oxford,

Bolingbroke, and the Duke of Ormond, were impeached for high treason; Oxford was sent to the Tower; Bolingbroke and Ormond escaped to the Continent, where they joined the councils of the Pretender. The Tory party, although out of official power, comprised the bulk of the landowners, the clergy, and the learning of England; and the popular mind—as shewn in tumultuous crowds, cheering Jacobite speeches, and burning effigies of King William—was largely reactionary.

As tidings of British agitation and discontent were wafted across the Channel, so rose the hopes of the Pretender and his little court of adherents at St. Germains. Vessels were equipped at Havre and Dieppe, with arms and ammunition. The Pretender's plan of operations turned upon the Duke of Ormond making a landing in England, and the Duke of Berwick in Scotland. The latter, a natural son of James II., by a sister of the Duke of Marlborough, had a high military reputation, and if he had had the general direction of the movement, the results might have been different. But on the 6th of September, 1715, the Earl of Mar, without any commission from the Pretender, set up his standard at Braemar, and proclaimed him King of Scotland.

Mar had got up Highland games and hunting expeditions, and being an eloquent speaker, he inflamed the minds of the chieftains with sanguine hopes of a successful issue to a general rising. Ten thousand men rallied round the flag of rebellion. And in Northumberland, under the Earl of Derwentwater, and Mr. Foster, a county member of Parliament, there was a simultaneous rising. Mar sent a thousand Highlandmen in aid; on their way they were joined by several noblemen and gentlemen of the south of Scotland. The little Northumbrian army marched into Lancashire, and occupied Preston; attacked there by royal troops, they, after an obstinate defence, surrendered.

Meanwhile, Mar, after occupying Perth, marched to join the English insurgents. At Sheriffmuir, near Dunblane, he was met by a royalist force under the Duke of Argyle, and on the same day as the surrender at Preston, a battle was fought. The left wing of both armies defeated its opponents; so it was technically a drawn battle. But it was tantamount to a rebel defeat; next morning Argyle occupied the field of action; Mar had retired to Perth. On December 22nd, the Pretender arrived in a small vessel at Peterhead. He made a quasi-royal progress to Perth, having himself proclaimed as James the Eighth in all the towns he passed through. Of a handsome person, he could be courteous in his manners; but he lacked animation; his general expression was sombre and uninviting, not one to raise enthusiasm in men engaged in a desperate enterprise. He entered Perth on 9th January, 1716, taking up his quarters at Scone, and giving instructions for his coronation.

But the dream of the crown, which had tantalized the prince from boyhood, vanished into thin air before the stern realities around him. Mar's army was dispirited by inaction, and melting away by desertions. Argyle had been reinforced by English troops and Dutch auxiliaries, and had had a field-train from Berwick. On January 30th, he was in sight of Perth. The prospect of a battle raised the spirits of the clansmen, but the leaders had seen for weeks that their enterprise was hopeless, and Mar ordered a retreat. It had been an especially cold winter, the Tay, instead of being a strongly flowing river, was then a frozen highway, and in sullen discontent, the clans crossed over and began their retreat. They marched in good order, unmolested by Argyle. In four days they had reached Montrose, *en route* for Aberdeen; there, it was

JAMES FRANCIS, THE OLD PRETENDER.

promised them they would meet a large body of French troops, and again, with bright hopes of success, march southwards.

On February 4th, the retreat was to be

continued; the carriage and mounted guards of the prince were waiting before the gateway of his lodgings, but no prince appeared. He had slunk off by a back-way and, with the Earl of Mar, Lord Drummond, and the *gentlemen* of his suite, gone on board a small vessel in the harbour, lying ready for their reception. It was, perhaps, the meanest desertion by the leaders of a warlike enterprise in all history. The prince left a sealed letter, to be opened in Aberdeen. Its contents were found to be formal thanks for faithful services, *permission* to choose between dispersion, and as a body coming to terms with the enemy; and apprizing the men that their pay had now ceased. There was an outburst of rage and mortification, and then the clans, under great privations, sought their native glens and villages; the leaders tried to make their escape to the continent from the northern sea-ports.

During the twelve years of Anne's reign there was not a single execution for treason, but now the headsman and hangman were again at work. Of those who took part in the English insurrection, the Earl of Derwentwater, Lord Kenmore, and about twenty other persons were executed. Foster and several others made rather marvellous escapes from prison. In Scotland about forty families of note lost their estates. But a trick of the government, in ordering that the commission for the trial of the Scottish rebels should sit in Carlisle, raised such a cry of injustice, and of being an infringement of the Articles of Union, that the accused were given to understand that if they did not challenge the authority of the Court, they would be mercifully dealt with. The result was, that although twenty-four were condemned, not one of them was executed.

After the native efforts of Jacobitism in 1715 had resulted in utter failure, it had certain glimmerings of success through foreign complications. King George never became in heart, in habits, or in policy, an Englishman. In his Hanoverian policy he embroiled Britain with Sweden and Spain. He purchased from the King of Denmark the duchies of Bremen and Verden, which duchies the King of Sweden—the redoubtable Charles XII.—claimed as his own. Charles now proposed to place himself at the head of a confederacy, to dethrone King George, and put the Pretender in his place. His idea was, to land with 10,000 men in the north of Scotland, to call upon the highland clans to again rally round a Jacobite standard, and, with the co-operation of a Spanish fleet, to march into England. It is one of the might-have-beens with which history abounds. But a cannon shot at the siege of Frederickshall, in 1718, ended the erratic course of Charles.

Next year the Pretender was received with royal honours at Madrid, and an expedition of ten ships of war, with 6,000 troops and much warlike stores on board, was placed under the command of the Duke of Ormond, and sailed for Scotland. A violent storm off Cape Finisterre scattered the expedition. Two frigates landed 300 men at Lewis; these surrendered to the royal troops sent against them. This same year the Pretender married a Polish princess; by her he had two sons,—Charles Edward, and Henry Benedict.

The Rebellion of 1745.

IN 1724, the government sent Marshal Wade into the Highlands to take measures to enforce law and order, and to facilitate military communication. Wade was a man of good common sense, and he did his work with tact and judgment. The clansmen were disarmed; but commissions were given to loyal chieftains to raise militia companies, to be disciplined and trained in the use of arms. Some of these companies, as the celebrated *Black Watch*, which became the 42nd regiment, were composed of men in good social positions, as farmers, tacksmen, and sons of highland gentlemen. And Wade employed his soldiers to construct, under skilful supervision, well-formed roads, connected together, and more direct. A memorable distich was posted up near Fort-William :—

"Had you seen those roads before they were made,
You would hold up your hands and bless General Wade."

On the surface the Highlands were quiet, and were being brought more and more within the pale of British citizenship. Sheriffs held their courts in all the northern shires; schools were established in every parish; farmers and breeders had better access to fairs and markets, and hillside cottars to their Kirks. But the embers of Jacobitism still smouldered; the chiefs had no liking for these German Georges, and the clansmen would still follow their chieftain's leadership.

But there was no special agitation or disquietude in the Highlands when, on the 25th of July, 1745, Prince Charles Edward landed on the south-west coast of Inverness-shire, and asked the neighbouring chiefs to join him in a new rebellion. He came, personally a stranger in the land, with a suite of seven gentlemen, to conquer a throne from which, fifty-seven years previously, his grandfather had been driven with ignominy and disgrace. There must have been a charm of person and manners in the prince—now in his twenty-fifth year—by which he won the hearts, and, even against their judgments, the enthusiastic support of the chiefs, who met him with the intention of persuading him to return to France. He lives in Scottish song and story as "Bonnie Prince Charlie"—the idol of the clansmen.

Some leading chiefs as MacDonald of Sleat

and MacLeod of MacLeod, declined to join the enterprise; but one man of foremost note—Cameron of Lochiel—declared for the prince, and sent out a gathering summons to arms. About

CHARLES EDWARD, THE YOUNG PRETENDER.

two thousand men saluted the standard when, on August 19th, it was set up at Glenfinnan. On the 3rd of September, the prince entered Perth; a fortnight later he was in Edinburgh. The magistrates had tried to organize a volunteer defence of the city; but when the words passed round, "the Highlanders are in sight," the gates were opened. But the castle held out for King George.

Sir John Cope, the Commander of the royal forces in Scotland had, at the news of the rebellion, gone with 1500 men into the Highlands; but, evading the prince's forces, he took shipping at Aberdeen, landed at Dunbar, and with reinforcements, marched on Edinburgh. The prince met him at Prestonpans, eight miles east of Edinburgh, and a battle was there fought on the morning of 21st September. The rush of the highlanders, with broadsword and target, here, as at Killiecrankie, carried the day. The royal troops were completely routed, and their artillery, baggage, and military chest fell to the victors.

The prince returned to Edinburgh amidst popular acclamations. His adventure had now assumed a more serious aspect. For a time it seemed as if the whole of Scotland,—except the castles of Edinburgh and Stirling, and the highland garrisons—was at his feet. Dundee and Perth were held by highland contingents; Glasgow was subjected to a payment of £5,000.

But it was six weeks before, from other highland clans coming in, and from lowland enlistments, his army mustered 5,500 men. At Holyrood balls and festivities, he courteously enacted the royal host. On October 31st, he began his march southwards, entering England by the western border. He took Carlisle, passed through Preston, Wigan, and Manchester, arriving at Derby on 4th December. The march was in two divisions; the front division was commanded by Lord George Murray, a thorough soldier in courage and ability. The rear division was led by the prince himself,—generally in highland garb, his target on his shoulder.

At Derby the prince might have said with Henry of Lancaster :—

"Thus far into the bowels of the land,
Have we marched on without impediment."

But what next—and next? A larger and better appointed army than his own, commanded by the Duke of Cumberland, was at Lichfield, only twenty-five miles to the south-west; another army, equal in numbers to his own, under Marshal Wade, was marching down on his rear through Yorkshire. The general opinion of a Council of War was for retreat. The prince at first refused his assent; he sulked over it for a day, and then gave in with a bad grace, saying he would call no more Councils of War, but act entirely on his own judgment. Early next morning—the 6th of December—the cheerless retreat began.

The very audacity of the irruption into England fostered an idea in the minds of both friends and enemies that the prince had some secret but well-founded assurance of powerful support, which in due time would reveal itself. But the idea was seen to be baseless when the highland brogues began to retrace the northern roads. In passing through Manchester on the march, there had been bonfires, acclamations, hand-kissing, and a display of white cockades. Ten days later, in the retreat, there was in Manchester a mob-demonstration against the highlanders; when they left the town, their rear guard was hooted and fired upon.

When the Duke of Cumberland learned of the retreat of the rebels, he hastened against them with all his cavalry; but their rear-guard, under Lord George Murray, gallantly repelled all attacks; and on 20th December, the prince's army was again on Scottish ground. After

LORD LOVAT.
From a drawing made by Hogarth the morning before his Lordship's execution.

levying contributions on Glasgow and Dumfries, he proceeded towards Stirling, making the historical village of Bannockburn his headquarters. Here he was joined by considerable reinforcements, including the clans Frazer, Farquharson, MacKenzie, and Macintosh. Simon, Lord Lovat, the aged chief of the Frazers, had been playing fast and loose, negotiating with the Prince for a dukedom as the price of his support; at the same time assuring the government of his loyalty, and asking for arms to enable his clan to act against the rebels. In the end, he sent his son with 750 Frazers to join the prince's standard; the crafty old fox himself remaining at home in pretended neutrality. By the middle of January the prince's muster-roll reached its maximum— about 8,500 men.

The prince had opened trenches for a regular siege of Stirling Castle, when he learned that General Hawley with 8,000 men, most of them veterans from the French wars, was marching against him. Lord George Murray—knowing that with such an army as that of the rebels, the chances of success lay more in attack than defence —made a rapid march on Hawley. On the afternoon of January 17th, a battle was fought on

Falkirk Moor. It was a wild fight, in a blinding storm of wind and rain. The darkening mists prevented combined operations on both sides. Divisions of each army drove back their immediate opponents, but themselves got into disorder in pursuit. Hawley in belief of defeat, fired his tents, fell back on Linlithgow, and next morning took his army to Edinburgh.

After the battle of Falkirk, the prince was for continuing the siege, but such plodding work did not suit the Highlanders, and the chiefs addressed a memorandum to him, advising retreat. He fumed and protested, but had again to yield. On February 4th, the Forth was forded, and the retreat began ; it was a leisurely one, no royalist force of any magnitude being in the Highlands. Inverness was occupied by the prince on February 18th. Forts George and Augustus surrendered ; Lord Loudon took what royalist troops he could collect into Ross-shire, where they were joined by the Whig Mac-Donalds.

The Duke of Cumberland came to Edinburgh, and organized an army. In addition to his British troops, 6,000 Hessians were landed at Leith. The army marched by Perth to

Aberdeen. On the 8th of April, the Duke left Aberdeen; on the 14th, he was at Nairn, 16 miles north of Inverness. His troops numbered 9,000 men,—a compact, well-fed, well-disciplined army, with full confidence in their leader, as a man of courage and large military experience.

The prince had not expected that the duke would leave Aberdeen before May, and his troops were scattered about. They had been for weeks in a state of semi-starvation, and had to roam the country to find food for a bare subsistence. The men were discontented for lack of pay; the leaders were jealous and suspicious of each other; some of the clans claimed special rights and precedences. It was a divided, a disheartened, almost a demoralized army of 7,000 men which, on April 15th, stood, with barely one ration for each man in the commissariat, upon Culloden Moor, about four miles north-east of Inverness.

Unequally matched as the two armies would have been if they had met on the 15th, they were much more so on the next day, when the battle joined. For in the intervening night, a strategical misadventure prostrated the spirit and weakened the efficiency of the prince's army. There was

THE REBELLION OF 1745.

an abortive attempt at a night attack on the royalist camp. After a long weary march, the rebel army failed to concentrate in time for a night surprise; and, disheartened and fatigued, it marched back to Culloden Moor. Here, many at once lay down to sleep, others scattered in search of food. At noon of the 16th, the two armies confronted each other.

Lord George Murray was watching for the proper moment to attack, but, without waiting for orders, the clans in the centre and right wings rushed down with their broadswords, and in spite of a galling fire broke through the front line of the enemy. But the second line had been trained to resist a Highland onset; they reserved their fire until the clansmen had almost reached the points of the bayonets, and then it told with deadly effect. The broadswords could not penetrate the steady line of bayonets; for the assailants it was either flight or death.

The three MacDonald regiments had been placed in the left wing of the rebel army. They claimed the right wing, and even in the supreme moment of battle, Highland pride predominated over military duty. They did not respond to the order to advance, and retired upon the second line. And now, a boundary wall on the prince's right had been thrown down by the Argyleshire Campbells, and a way made for the duke's cavalry to operate on the flank and rear. His main army advanced in compact order, and it became a panic, and "save himself who can," with the clansmen. The MacDonalds and a portion of the second line retired in fair order; but the duke's cavalry cut off all stragglers; and all the wounded rebels on the battlefield, even those who were next morning found alive, were—by the duke's orders it is said—savagely put to death.

And not with the fever-madness of battle did the savageries terminate. Cumberland had at Carlisle, where the prince had unwisely left a small garrison, begun a course of atrocity; and he now went over the Highlands, a very demon of cruelty and destruction. This prince of the blood-royal of England gave his soldiery licence to shoot in cold blood the male inhabitants, to plunder the houses of the chieftains, to drive off the cattle and burn the huts of the peasants; to outrage the women. His ducal title ought to have died with him; for what man of honour or common humanity but would feel it a disgrace to bear an appellation made for ever infamous by the *Butcher of Culloden* ?

And the penalties of law supplemented the work of the sword. Lords Kilmarnock, Balmerino and Lovat, were beheaded on Tower Hill,—the last deaths by decapitation in Britain. About a

THE BLOCK, ETC., TOWER OF LONDON.

hundred persons were hanged in Scotland, and fifty in England ; hundreds were sent to the plantations. Of course it had been rebellion, but so far as the rebels were concerned, it had been a fair, stand-up fight ; they had lost all but honour. They had not been robbers, or guilty of violence towards civilians ; they had not maltreated their prisoners, but set them free on parole, which was often broken. Humanity and sound policy might well have spoken for mercy.

When the prince saw the enemy closing in upon his broken host, he may have hesitated whether he should not stand and meet death, sword in hand; but his friends took hold of his horse's bridle and turned it from the field. With few attendants he rode to Castle Downie, the residence of Lord Lovat. On seeing the prince a fugitive, the crafty old man felt the ground trembling under his own feet; so the prince had only a hasty meal, and again rode on. He passed by Invergarry into the West Highlands; there, and in the Western Isles, he was for over five months a hunted outlaw. Government offered a reward of £30,000 for his capture; yet, although one time and another hundreds knew of his whereabouts, not one of these grasped at this, to them, fabulous amount, through treachery. But the soldiery and unfriendly clansmen were vigilantly on the outlook.

The prince had, in his wanderings, gone to the outer Hebrides, and was lodged in a forester's hut, in a cleft of the hills. General Campbell landed at South Uist to make a minute search of the islands. The MacDonalds of Skye were also there, engaged in the same task,—a hunt-party of two thousand men. We can imagine the avidity of the search—the warrant for a huge fortune

FLORA MACDONALD.
From a painting by Ramsay.

might be found under any bracken bush on the hillside,—within any clump of trees, or beneath any overhanging cliff. When escape seemed impossible, a woman's compassion and a woman's wit came to the rescue.

No feminine name is in Scotland more honoured or awakens higher thoughts of courage and devotion than that of Flora MacDonald. She belonged to the MacDonalds who were inimical to the prince, and was—when she came to know of his straits—on a visit to the house of Sir Alexander MacDonald. But she boldly asked the chief for a passport for herself, a man-servant, and a maid-servant, to enable her to visit relatives in a neighbouring island. The prince, dressed up as maid "Bridget," shewed awkward enough, but without detection the party reached the house of MacDonald of Kingsburgh, to whom Flora was afterwards married. From there the prince again reached the mainland.

Here he had, in a closely-watched district, several hair-breadth escapes, and found that misery *does* acquaint a man with strange bed-fellows! One refuge was a robber's cave, the other occupants being outlawed cattle-stealers. They knew the prince, and treated him with the same loyal respect as, ten months previously, had been shewn him in the halls of Holyrood. He was at length able to join Lochiel and other outlawed adherents. Friends along the coast were watching for a French vessel. One appearing on September 20th, nearly a hundred persons were safely embarked. The prince is described as looking like the spectre of his former self,—pale, haggard, and ragged. But his companions received him with bonnets doffed and loyal salutations. Although chased by an English cruiser, the vessel got safely to Marlaix, in Brittany.

Index.

Aberdeen, Old, 152; Candlemas procession in, 153; reception of James IV. in, 153; church utensils, public sale of, 156; English players in, 157; early closing of taverns at, 158; fines for non-attendance at church, 158; trials for witchcraft in, 164
Act of Security, The, 272
Administration of effects, Provisions for the, 149
Agricola in Britain, 4
Alaric takes Rome, 10
Alexander III., King, 41
Alfred, King, Danish conflicts of, 39
Angles give their name to South Britain, 19
Anglican Church, Origin of the, 88
Anglo-Saxon Heptarchy, The, 21
Anne, Queen, reign of, 672; her domestic history, 279; favours the Pretender, 280; her death, 281
Argyle, Earl of, sentenced to death, 231; his insurrection, 240; execution of, 241
Argyle, Marquis of, his execution, 212
Arminius defeats the Romans, 10
Assembly, General, in Glasgow, 182
Assembly of Divines in Westminster, 192
Athelstane, King, 41
Augustine, Mission of, 22

Baliol nominated King by Edward I., 65
Barons' sons, The education of, 114
Battle of Bannockburn, 71
,, Brunanberg, 41
,, Culloden, 299
,, Drumclog, 223
,, Dunbar, 200
,, Falkirk, 297
,, Hastings, 53

Battle of Killiecrankie, 261
,, Prestonpans, 292
,, Sedgemoor, 237
,, Sheriff-muir, 283
,, Stamford Bridge, 53
,, The Standard, 58
,, Worcester, 203
Beaton, Cardinal, Murder of, 90
Berwick, The Duke of, 282
Bishops, Seven, Arrest and Trial of, 250
Bishops, *Tulchan*, in Scotland, 179
"Black Watch," Composition of the, 289
"Bloody Assize," The, 238
Boadicea, Queen, defeated by the Romans, 4
Boot, Torture of the, 218
Borders, The, long disorderly, 77
Bothwell Bridge, Battle of, 225; cruel treatment of prisoners taken at, 227
Bretwalda, an Anglo-Saxon dignity, 21
Britain, Invasion of, by Julius Cæsar, 1; the second invasion and conquest, 3; as a Roman province, 12; the Roman evacuation, 16; barbarian raids on, 17; the Anglo-Saxons in, 19; Danish invasions of, 38
British Churches, Ancient, differences between, 24
Brown, John, Cruel murder of, 228
Bruce, Robert, his contest for the crown, 68; his army before Stirling, 69; his victory at Bannockburn, 72
Burgh Court of Dundee, old records of, 134; justice done in the, 135; assumed powers of life and death, 141

Cæsar, Julius, Invasion of Britain by, 2

INDEX.

Caledonians, The, 5
Candlemas procession in Aberdeen, 153
Canongate, The, its old memories, 124
Canute, The Danish King, 46
Caractacus defeated by the Romans, 4
Catholic church utensils, Sale of, 156
Catholic conversions under James II., 245
Catholic worship, Stringent laws against, 116
Celtic Language, The, 9
Celts, Origin of the, 27
Channel, Revolution expedition in the, 254
Charles I., Scotland under, 178; endeavours to subvert Presbyterianism, 179; his game of *Thorough*, 184; at war with Parliament, 191; joins the Scottish army, 195; given up to Parliamentary army, 196; at Carisbrook Castle, 197
Charles II. signs the Covenant, 199; is crowned at Scone, 201; defeated at Worcester, 203; the Restoration, 211; Scotland under, 213; establishes Episcopacy, 214; his death, 235
Charles Edward, Prince, lands in Scotland, 290; in Edinburgh, 291; in Derby, 293; at Culloden, 298; wanderings and escape, 302
Charles XII. of Sweden designs invading Britain, 287
Churches, Ancient British, 24
Civilization, Modern turning point in, 85
Civil War, The, 191
Claverhouse, Graham of, 223; defeated at Drumclog, 224; his cruel revenge, 226; raises Highland clans in Jacobite cause, 260; his death at Killiecrankie, 262
Columba settles in Iona, 32
Commission to discuss terms of Union, 273
Constantius, The Emperor, 7
Constantine, The Emperor, 8

Conversion of the Anglo-Saxons, 22
Conversion of the Picts, 33
Cope, Sir John, defeated at Prestonpans, 292
"Covenant," Origin of the, 91
Covenanters at Rullion Green, 217; at Drumclog, 223; at Bothwell Bridge, 225; persecutions of, 227; martyrs' monument in Greyfriars' churchyard, 247
Cromwell in Scotland, 199; wins battle of Dunbar, 200; Scotland under, 206; his latter days, 207; his character, 207
Culdees, The, 33
Culloden, The Rebel army at, 298; the battle, 299; atrocities after the battle, 300
Cumberland, Duke of, follows retreat of Rebel army from Derby, 294; marches against the Rebels, 297; wins battle of Culloden, 299; his savagery, 300
Cures from holy wells, 167

Dalrida, Scoto, Kingdom of, 31
Dalziel persecutes the Covenanters, 216
Danish invasions of Britain, The, 38
Darien Scheme, The, 270; ends in disaster, 271
Darnley, Lord, marries Queen Mary, 107; his murder, 108
David I., King, 58
Declaration of Indulgence, The, 248
Declaration of Rights, The, 258
"Defender of the Faith," Title of, 87
Derby, March of Rebels to, 293; retreat from, 294
Derwentwater, Earl of, raises a rebellion, 283
Dress regulations in Sixteenth Century, 150
Druidism in Britain, 13
Drumclog, Battle of, 223
Drummond, Sir William, 83; his welcome of Charles I. to Edinburgh, 178
Drunkenness, Punishments for, 145
Dunbar, Battle of, 200
Dunbar's description of pageant in Aberdeen, 153
Duncan, King, 55

INDEX.

Dundee, History of Old, 134; Burgh Court records, 135; offences and punishments, 136; stormed by General Monk, 204
Dunottar Castle, Siege of, 128

Edgar the Peaceable, 42
Edinburgh, Old, 111; a picturesque city, 112; early history of, 112; provisions against fire, 113; early schools, 114; after Flodden, 114; Mary's entrance into, 117; quarrel of James VI. with, 120; James revisits, 122; resistance to episcopacy in, 182; occupied by Prince Charles Edward, 292
Edinburgh Castle, 126; an ancient royal residence, 127; the regalia in, 127
Edward, King, the elder, 40
Edward the Confessor, 48
Edward I., arbitrator on claims to Scottish crown, 64; decides for Baliol, 65; conquers Scotland, 66; his death, 68
Edward II. invades Scotland, 69; is defeated at Bannockburn, 71
Effects, Administration of, 149
Elizabeth becomes Queen of England, 105; her hatred of Mary, 106; causes Mary's execution, 109: comparison of the two queens, 109
Ella, Landing of, 19
Emma, Queen, 46
England and Scotland, Strained relations between, 273; Union of, 276
English, Preparation against attacks by the, 155
English Reformation, Causes of the, 86
English and Scottish Churches, Difference between, 90
English and Scottish Parliaments, Different constitution of, 74
Episcopacy introduced into Scotland by Charles I., 179
Ethelbert, Conversion of, 22
Ethelred the Unready, 44

Falkirk, Battle of, 299
Feudalism in Britain, 73
Field-preaching in Scotland, 214

Folk-speech, Scottish, 84
Foster, Mr., heads a Jacobite rising, 283

Gaelic language, The, 29
Geddes, Jenny, throws her stool, 180
George I., Accession of, 281
Glasgow, General assembly in, 182; fined by Prince Charles Edward, 296
Glencoe, Massacre of, 264; resolution on by the Scottish estates, 269
Godwin, Earl, 48; his banishment, 49; his return, 50
Graham of Claverhouse, 223
Grampians, Battle of the, 5

Halley, General, defeated at Falkirk, 297
"Hand-fasting" in Scotland, 173
Hardicanute, King, 47
Harold, Earl, maltreated by William of Normandy, 50; his high character, 51; chosen king, 52; defeats the Norsemen at Stamford Bridge, 53; defeated and slain at Hastings, 54
Hastings, Battle of, 54
Henry VIII., his domestic history, 86; his evil character, 87; effects the English Reformation, 88; demands Mary for his son's wife, 102
Heptarchy, The Anglo-Saxon, 21
Heresy (Lutheran), Act of Parliament against, 155
Highlanders mode of fighting, 261; advance into England, 293; in retreat, 294
"Highland Host, The," 220
Highlands long disorderly, 76; under General Wade, 289
Holyrood, History of, 129; Queen Mary's apartments in, 130; gallery of ancient kings in, 35; the church, 132
Holy Wells in Scotland, 166; associated with certain saints, 167; pilgrimages to, 167; at St. Fillans, 168; at Musselburgh, 168; at Muthill near Crieff, 169; at Strathnaven, 169; at Spa near Aberdeen,

170; pilgrimages to denounced by the Strathbogie Presbytery, 170

Ill-fame, Houses of, forbidden, 148
Images in churches, Demolition of, 99
Immorality, Penalties for, 145
Indulgence, Declaration of, 248
Inverness occupied by the rebels, 297
Iona, Historical importance of, 33
Ireland, The old races in, 30; Patrick's mission in, 32
Irish troops in London, 252

Jacobite risings in 1715, 279
James I., his high character, 78; a poet, 82; his wise laws, 113
James III. patronises poets, 129
James IV. and Sir David Lindsay, 130; his entry with his queen into Edinburgh, 114; into Aberdeen, 153
James V. dying at Mary's birth, 102
James VI., proclaimed king, 118; supposed to be under witchcraft, 161; quarrels with Edinburgh, 120; becomes James I. of England, 122; revisits Edinburgh, 123; his method of arguing with the Puritans, 185
James, Duke of York, fights the Dutch at sea, 236; in Scotland, 230; as king attempts to re-establish popery, 242; issues the declaration of indulgence, 248; sends seven bishops to the Tower, 249; has a son born, 250; retracts unpopular measures, 253; his flight, 255: his throne declared vacant, 257; Scotland under, 246;
James the Pretender joins the rising of 1715, 284; makes arrangements for his coronation, 284; deserts his adherents, 286
Jeffreys, the infamous Judge, 232, 238
Jougs, The, 149
Justice, Good, done in Burgh Courts, 135
Jutes first landing in Britain, 17

Kenneth Macalpine, King of Scots, 36
Killiecrankie, Battle of, 261
"Kings' Quhair, The," 81
Knox, John, his early life, 91; preaching at Perth, 92; admonishes Queen Mary, 96; his strong character, 98

Landowners bound for their tenants attending church, 220
Latin a spoken language in Britain, 8
Lauderdale, Persecutions of Lord, 219
Lent observances after the Reformation, 157
Leslie, General, at Dunbar, 200
Lindsay, Sir David, 130
Lisle, Alice, Execution of, 238
Literature, The older Scottish, 80
Lochiel, Adherence of to Prince Charles, 291
Logarithms, Invention of, by Napier, 123
Long Parliament, The, 190
Lothians, People of the, 80
Lovat, Lord, his double dealing, 296; his execution, 301
Lowland folk-speech, 84
Luther's heresies, An act against, 155

Macbeth, King, 55
Macdonald, Flora, aids the escape of Prince Charles, 304
Macdonalds of Glencoe, Order to extirpate the, 267; treacherous murders of, 268
Macdonalds, The, at Culloden, 299
MacIan of Glencoe, 265; takes the oath of allegiance, 266; his murder, 268
Mackay, General, defeated at Killiecrankie, 261
Magus Muir, Tragedy of, 222
Maid of Norway, The, 64
"Maiden," The, 119
Malcolm II., King, 54
Malcolm, III., *Canmore*, 56; marries Margaret, sister of Edgar Atheling, 57
Malcolm IV., *The Maiden*, 59
Mar, Earl of, raises a rebellion in 1715, 282; is checked at Sheriffmuir, 283; deserts his army at Montrose, 286

INDEX.

Margaret, queen of Malcolm Canmore, 57
Marriage, Scottish customs, 172; lax notions on, 174; restrictions on, 175; unlucky months for, 172; a woman's outfit, 175
Mary of Guise, regent of Scotland, 90
Mary, Queen of England, 104
Mary, Queen of Scots, Childhood of, 102; sent to France, and marries the Dauphin, 103; returns to Scotland, 116; her entry into Edinburgh, 117; marries Lord Darnley, 106; her sad after-history, 109; compared with Elizabeth, 110; her apartments in Holyrood, 130
Masham, Mrs., Influence of over Queen Anne, 279
Massacre of Glencoe, The, 264
McKail, Hugh, Execution of, 218
Monmouth, Duke of, defeats the Covenanters at Bothwell Bridge, 225; his Moderation, 226; his own Rebellion, 237
Monk, General, storms Dundee; 204; completes Cromwell's subjugation of Scotland, 206; restores the Stuarts, 211
"Mons Meg" at Edinburgh Castle, 126
Montrose, the Marquis of, 194
Morton, Regent of Scotland, 118; accused of being accessory to Darnley's murder, 118: his execution by the *Maiden*, 119
Murray, Lord George, leads the rebel march to Derby in 1745, 293
Musselburgh, Holy-well at, 168

Napier of Merchiston invents logarithms, 123
Nationalism, English and Scottish, 81
Newcastle held by the Scots, 183
Night offences specially punished, 139
Normandy a Danish Conquest, 44
Norsemen hold North of Scotland, 54
Northumbria the chief power, 23

Offences and their punishments in the sixteenth century, 134
Oswald, King of Northumbria, becomes *Bretwalda*, 23; his conversion, 23
Oxford declares for the royal supremacy, 244; is "hoist by its own petard," 244
Oysters, penalty for giving false price to, 154

Parliament, The Long, 190
Parliament declares James's throne vacant, 257: agrees to William and Mary's joint sovereignty, 258
Parliaments in England and Scotland, 74
Paterson, William, floats the Darien scheme, 270; the total failure, 271
Patrick, the Saint of Ireland, 32
Penny Weddings, 173
Perth in Jacobite occupation in 1715, 283; the retreat from, 284
"Petition of Right," The, 184
Picts, first mention of the, 6; origin of the, 28; conversion of, 33; coalesce with the Scots, 36
Players, Reception of in Aberdeen, 157
Poetry, The older Scottish, 81
Pope, Henry VIII. quarrels with the, 88
Popery, Protestant intolerance towards, 116
Presbyterian Church of Scotland, distinctive features of, 94; its influence on Scottish character, 95; bareness of its forms of worship, 100; its fight against episcopacy, 181
Presbyterianism in England, 193
Prestonpans, Battle of, 292
Pretender, Birth of the, 250; in the rebellion of 1715, 284; birth of his two sons, 288
Protestantism established in England, 88; in Scotland, 92
"Protestant wind," A, watched for, 253
Psalms and paraphrases in the Kirk, 100
Punishments in the sixteenth

century, 135; for speaking falsely of burgh officers, 136; for slander, 136; for "flyting," 137; of having to pay for healing hurts, 138; of banishment from the town, 140; of scourging through the town, 141; of death under burgh laws, 141; of restitution, 142; when there was "vehement suspicion," 142; of forfeiting the right to wear swords, 143; for drunkenness, 145; for immorality, 148
Puritans, the English, 184; browbeaten by James I., 185; their Old Testament leanings, 208

Queen of Charles I., evil influence of, 186
Queens, The rival, Mary and Elizabeth, 102; their relationship, 105

Rebellion, Jacobite, of 1715, 283; Executions following the, 286
Rebellion of 1745, 289; atrocities and executions following, 300
Reformation, The, in England and Scotland, 85; in danger from James II., 242
Regalia, the ancient Scottish, 127; the present, 127; its adventures, 128; after the Union to remain in Edinburgh, 128; supposed loss, search for, and recovery, 128
Regencies disastrous to Scotland, 75
Regicides, Execution of the, 212
Religion in Scotland under Charles I., 181; under Cromwell, 209; under Charles II., 214;
Renwick, the last covenanting martyr, 248
Revolution, The, of 1688, 252
Rizzio, David, Murder of, 108
Roman invasion of Britain, 3; rule in Britain, 12; Empire divided, 9; fall of the Western Empire, 11; Evacuation, 16
Rome taken by Alaric, 10
Rullion Green, Fight at, 217
Russell, Sir William, Execution of, 233
Ryehouse Plot, The, 233

Sabbath-breaking, Penalties for, 158
Saints associated with Holy-wells, 167
"Saxon shore," The, 15
Scotia, an old name of Ireland, 29
Scotland, how it became a free nation, 63; under Charles I., 178; under Cromwell, 199; under Charles II., 211; under James II., 236; "Company of," 270; union with England, 270
Scottish Kings:—The Mythical, 35; Fergus, 35; Kenneth Macalpine, 36; Malcolm II., 54; Duncan, 55; Macbeth, 55; Malcolm III., 56; David I., 58; Malcolm IV., 59; William, 59; Alexander III., 61; Baliol, 65; Robert Bruce, 72; James I., 78, 81; James III., 129; James IV., 130; James VI., 116
Scottish Nation, Rise of the, 26; Parliament a single chamber, 74; Nobles, quarrels amongst, 75; Nationalism pronounced, 81; Reformation, a struggle with authority, 90; Convention declare James's throne vacant, 259
Scoto-Irish piracies, 15
Scots first found in Ireland, 29; lesser number of than of Picts, 36; "King of," the title of the sovereign, 72
"Security, Act of," 272
Sedgemoor, Battle of, 237
Sharp, Archbishop, Murder of, 221
Sheriff-Muir, Battle of, 283
Sheriffs in Scotland, Education of, 114
Shipmoney, Levy of, 187
Springs of mineral waters become holy wells, 167
St. Fillans, Well of, 168
St. Giles, The saint's statue in, removed, 115; farewell speech of James VI. in, 122; commotion in over new liturgy, 180
St. Mary's altar, Fines of lights for, 138
Stair, Master of, author of Glencoe massacre, 265; punished by dismissal from office, 269

INDEX.

Stamford Bridge, Battle of, 53
Standard, Battle of the, 58
Star-Chamber, The, 184
Stocks, Punishment of the, 138
Strafford, Execution of, 191
Strathbogie Presbytery denounce pilgrimages to holy wells, 170
Strathclyde, Kingdom of, 21
Strathnaven, Holy well at, 169
Stuarts, Family traits of the, 213; their claims to the English throne, 105; the last act of the dynasty, 281
Superstition, Hard death of, 160
Swearing, Penalties for, 147
Sweden, Charles XII. of, 287
Sweyn, The Danish King, 45
Swords, Wearing of, led to crime, 143; disallowed after misuse, 144

Test Oaths in Scotland, Evasion of, 245
Teutonic rule, Spread of the, 18
"Thorough," The game of, 184
Tory ministry of Queen Anne, 281
Treason, English laws of, applied to Scotland, 276
Tulchan bishops in Scotland, 179

Union of England and Scotland, William's dying message in favour of, 272; its terms, 274;
opposition to in Scotland, 275; its accomplishment, 276; early years of the, 276; attempts to repeal the, 277; its good results, 278

Wade, General, in the Highlands, 289
Wallace, Sir William, 67
War, The Civil, 191
Wedding Feasts in Scotland, 172
Westminster Assembly of Divines, The, 192
William the Conqueror, 52
William, Prince of Orange, invitation to, 252; his fleet in the Channel, 254; his landing and progress, 254; refuses the regency, 257; elected King and his wife Queen, 258; his tolerant policy, 262; signs order against the Macdonalds of Glencoe, 266; opposes the Darien Scheme, 271; his last message to Parliament, 272
Witchcraft in Scotland, 160; in Aberdeen, 164
Witches, An assize on in Edinburgh, 161
Witchfinders, 163
"Woo'd and married and a'" 176

York, Early importance of, 7

PUBLICATIONS
OF
WILLIAM ANDREWS & CO.,
THE HULL PRESS,
HULL.

SECOND EDITION. *Bound in cloth gilt, demy 8vo.* 6s

Curiosities of the Church:

Studies of Curious Customs, Services, and Records,

By WILLIAM ANDREWS, F.R.H.S.,

AUTHOR OF "HISTORIC ROMANCE," "FAMOUS FROSTS AND
FROST FAIRS," "HISTORIC YORKSHIRE," ETC.

CONTENTS:

Early Religious Plays: being the Story of the English Stage in its Church Cradle Days—The Caistor Gad-Whip Manorial Service—Strange Serpent Stories—Church Ales—Rush-Bearing—Fish in Lent—Concerning Doles—Church Scrambling Charities—Briefs—Bells and Beacons for Travellers by Night—Hour Glasses in Churches—Chained Books in Churches—Funeral Effigies—Torchlight Burials—Simple Memorials of the Early Dead—The Romance of Parish Registers—Dog Whippers and Sluggard Wakers—Odd Items from Old Accounts—A carefully compiled Index.

ILLUSTRATED.

Press Opinions.

" A volume both entertaining and instructive, throwing much light on the manners and customs of bygone generations of Churchmen, and will be read to-day with much interest."—*Newbery House Magazine.*

" An extremely interesting volume."—*North British Daily Mail.*

" A work of lasting interest."—*Hull Examiner.*

" The reader will find much in this book to interest, instruct, and amuse."—*Home Chimes.*

" We feel sure that many will feel grateful to Mr. Andrews for having produced such an interesting book."—*The Antiquary.*

" A volume of great research and striking interest."—*The Bookbuyer (New York).*

" A valuable book."—*Literary World (Boston, U.S.A.).*

" An admirable book."—*Sheffield Independent.*

" An interesting, handsomely got up volume. . . . Mr. Andrews is always chatty and expert in making a paper on a dry subject exceedingly readable."—*Newcastle Courant.*

" Mr. William Andrews' new book, 'Curiosities of the Church,' adds another to the series by which he has done so much to popularise antiquarian studies. . . . The book, it should be added, has some qu..int illustrations, and its rich matter is made available for reference by a full and carefully compiled index."—*Scotsman.*

HULL: WILLIAM ANDREWS & CO., THE HULL PRESS.
London: Hutchinson & Co.

Elegantly bound in cloth gilt, demy 8vo., price 6s.

Old Church Lore.

By WILLIAM ANDREWS, F.R.H.S.,

Author of "Curiosities of the Church," "Old-Time Punishments," "Historic Romance," etc.

CONTENTS.

The Right of Sanctuary—The Romance of Trial—A Fight between the Mayor of Hull and the Archbishop of York—Chapels on Bridges—Charter Horns—The Old English Sunday—The Easter Sepulchre—St. Paul's Cross—Cheapside Cross—The Biddenden Maids Charity—Plagues and Pestilences—A King Curing an Abbot of Indigestion—The Services and Customs of Royal Oak Day—Marrying in a White Sheet—Marrying under the Gallows—Kissing the Bride—Hot Ale at Weddings—Marrying Children—The Passing Bell—Concerning Coffins—The Curfew Bell—Curious Symbols of the Saints—Acrobats on Steeples—A carefully-prepared Index.

ILLUSTRATED

PRESS OPINIONS.

"A worthy work on a deeply interesting subject. . . . We commend this book strongly."—*European Mail.*

"An interesting volume."—*The Scotsman.*

"Contains much that will interest and instruct."—*Glasgow Herald.*

"The author has produced a book which is at once entertaining and valuable, and which is also entitled to unstinted praise on the ground of its admirable printing and binding."—*Shields Daily Gazette.*

"Mr. Andrews' book does not contain a dull page. . . . Deserves to meet with a very warm welcome."—*Yorkshire Post.*

"Mr. Andrews, in 'Old Church Lore,' makes the musty parchments and records he has consulted redolent with life and actuality, and has added to his works a most interesting volume, which, written in a light and easy narrative style, is anything but of the 'dry-as-dust' order. The book is handsomely got up, being both bound and printed in an artistic fashion."—*Northern Daily News.*

HULL: WILLIAM ANDREWS & CO., THE HULL PRESS.
London: Hutchinson & Co.

Elegantly bound in cloth gilt, crown quarto, price 10s. 6d.

Old=Time Punishments.

By WILLIAM ANDREWS, F.R.H.S.,

AUTHOR OF "CURIOSITIES OF THE CHURCH," "HISTORIC ROMANCE," "FAMOUS FROSTS AND FROST FAIRS," "HISTORIC YORKSHIRE," ETC.

CONTENTS.

Carefully prepared papers, profusely illustrated, appear on the following subjects:—

The Ducking Stool—The Brank, or Scold's Bridle—The Pillory—Punishing Authors and burning books—Finger-Pillory—The Jougs—The Stocks—The Drunkard's Cloak—Whipping—Public Penance in White Sheets—The Repentance-Stool—Riding the Stang—Gibbet Lore—Drowning—Burning to Death—Boiling to Death—Beheading—Hanging, Drawing, and Quartering—Pressing to Death—Hanging—Hanging in Chains—The Halifax Gibbet—The Scottish Maiden, etc.—An Index of five closely-printed pages.

MANY CURIOUS ILLUSTRATIONS.

PRESS OPINIONS.

"This is an entertaining book . . . well-chosen illustrations and a serviceable index."—*Athenæum*.
"A hearty reception may be bespoken for it."—*Globe*.
"A work which will be eagerly read by all who take it up."—*Scotsman*.
"It is entertaining."—*Manchester Guardian*.
"A vast amount of curious and entertaining matter."—*Sheffield Independent*.
"We can honestly recommend a perusal of this book."—*Yorkshire Post*.
"Interesting and handsomely printed."—*Newcastle Chronicle*.
"A very readable history."—*Birmingham Daily Gazette*.
"Mr. Andrews' book is well worthy of careful study, and is a perfect mine of wealth on the subject of which it treats."—*Herts Advertiser*.
"It is sure of a warm welcome on both sides of the Atlantic."—*Christian Leader*.

HULL: WILLIAM ANDREWS & CO., THE HULL PRESS.
London: Hutchinson & Co.

Elegantly bound in cloth gilt, demy 8vo., price 6s.

Bygone England:

Social Studies in its Historic Byways and Highways.

By WILLIAM ANDREWS, F.R.H.S.,

Author of "*Old Church Lore*," "*Curiosities of the Church*," "*Old Time Punishments*," *etc.*

Contents:

Under Watch and Ward.
  Under Lock and Key.
    The Practice of Pledging.
The Minstrel in the Olden Time.
  Curious Landholding Customs.
    Curiosities of Slavery in England.
Buying and Selling in the Olden Time.
  Curious Fair Customs.
    Old Prejudices against Coal.
The Sedan Chair.
  Running Footmen.
    The Early Days of the Umbrella.
A Talk about Tea.
  Concerning Coffee.
    The Horn Book.
Fighting Cocks in Schools.
  Bull-Baiting.
    The Badge of Poverty.
Patents to wear Nightcaps.
  A Foolish Fashion.
    Wedding Notices in the Last Century.
Selling Wives.
  The Story of the Tinder Box.
    The Invention of Friction Matches.
Body Snatching.
  Christmas under the Commonwealth.
    Under the Mistletoe Bough.
  A carefully prepared Index.

NUMEROUS ILLUSTRATIONS.

Opinions of the Press.

The following are a few extracts from a large number of favourable reviews of "Bygone England":—

"We welcome 'Bygone England.' It is another of Mr. Andrews' meritorious achievements in the path of popularising archæological and old-time information without in any way writing down to an ignoble level."—*The Antiquary.*

"This is a book which will give instruction as well as entertainment to all who read it, and it will serve to awaken interest in the old and quaint customs of our native land."—*Sala's Journal.*

"The volume is admirably got up, and its contents are at once entertaining and instructive. Mr. Andrews is quite a master of curious and out-of-the-way knowledge."—*Scottish Leader.*

"'A delightful book,' is the verdict that the reader will give after a perusal of its pages. Mr. Andrews has presented to us in very pleasing form some phases of the social life of England in the olden time."—*Publishers' Circular.*

"Some of the chapters are very interesting, and are most useful for those who desire to know the origin and history of some of our daily practices and amusements."—*The World.*

"In recommending this book to the general public, we do so, feeling confident that within its pages they will find much that is worth knowing, that they will never find their interest flag, nor their curiosity ungratified."—*Hull Daily News.*

"A volume which may be cordially recommended to all who love to stray in historical byways."—*Shields Daily Gazette.*

"A very readable and instructive volume."—*The Globe.*

"Many are the subjects of interest introduced in this chatty volume."—*Saturday Review.*

"A delightful volume for all who love to dive into the origin of social habits and customs, and to penetrate into the byways of history."—*Liverpool Daily Post.*

"There is a large mass of information in this capital volume, and it is so pleasantly put that many will be tempted to study it. Mr. Andrews has done his work with great skill."—*London Quarterly Review.*

"It is impossible to read this book without a feeling of gratitude to Mr. Andrews for his labours. The subjects have been so well selected, and are treated in so attractive a manner, that the reader may open the volume at any page and find something which will rivet his attention. . . . A good index is provided, and the book is well printed and got up."—*Manchester Examiner.*

"This informing and readable book will be welcome in any household."—*Yorkshire Post.*

Hull : **William Andrews & Co., The Hull Press.**
London: **Hutchinson & Co.**

AN IMPORTANT BOOK FOR REFERENCE.

Fcap. 4to. Bevelled boards, gilt tops. Price 4s.

FAMOUS FROSTS AND FROST FAIRS
IN GREAT BRITAIN.
Chronicled from the Earliest to the Present Time.

By WILLIAM ANDREWS, F.R.H.S.,
Author of "BYGONE ENGLAND," "CURIOSITIES OF THE CHURCH," "OLD-TIME PUNISHMENTS," ETC.

Only 400 copies printed, each copy numbered, and only 20 remain on sale. Three curious full-page illustrations.

THIS work furnishes a carefully prepared account of all the great Frosts occurring in this country from A.D. 134 to 1887. The numerous Frost Fairs on the Thames are fully described, and illustrated with quaint woodcuts, and several old ballads relating to the subject are reproduced. It is tastefully printed and elegantly bound.

The following are a few of the many favourable reviews of "Famous Frosts and Frost Fairs":—

"The work is thoroughly well written, it is careful in its facts, and may be pronounced exhaustive on the subject. Illustrations are given of several frost fairs on the Thames, and as a trustworthy record this volume should be in every good library. The usefulness of the work is much enhanced by a good index."—*Public Opinion.*

"The book is beautifully got up."—*Barnsley Independent.*

"A very interesting volume."—*Northern Daily Telegraph.*

"A great deal of curious and valuable information is contained in these pages. . . . A comely volume."—*Literary World.*

"The work from first to last is a most attractive one, and the arts alike of printer and binder have been brought into one to give it a pleasing form."—*Wakefield Free Press.*

"An interesting and valuable work."—*West Middlesex Times.*

"Not likely to fail in interest."—*Manchester Guardian.*

"This chronology has been a task demanding extensive research and considerable labour and patience, and Mr. Andrews is to be heartily congratulated on the result."—*Derby Daily Gazette.*

"A volume of much interest and great importance."—*Rotherham Advertiser.*

HULL: WILLIAM ANDREWS & CO., THE HULL PRESS.
LONDON: HUTCHINSON & Co.

Elegantly bound in cloth gilt, demy 8vo, price 7s. 6d.

Only 500 copies printed, and each copy numbered. Only 30 copies remain on sale.

BYGONE NORTHAMPTONSHIRE:

Its History, Folk-Lore, and Memorable Men and Women.

Edited by WILLIAM ANDREWS, F.R.H.S.,

Author of "BYGONE ENGLAND," "OLD-TIME PUNISHMENTS," "CURIOSITIES OF THE CHURCH," "OLD CHURCH LORE."

Contents:—Historic Northamptonshire, by Thomas Frost—The Eleanor Crosses, by the Rev. Geo. S. Tyack, B.A.—Fotheringhay: Past and Present, by Mrs. Dempsey—The Battle of Naseby, by Edward Lamplough—The Cottage Countess—The Charnel House at Rothwell, by Edward Chamberlain—The Gunpowder Plot, by John T. Page—Earls Barton Church, by T. Tindall Wildridge—Old Fairs, by William Sharman—Witches and Witchcraft, by Eugene Teesdale—The City of Peterborough, by Frederick Ross, F.R.H.S.—The English Founders of the Washington Family of America, by Thomas Frost—Ann Bradstreet, the Earliest American Poetess—Liber Custumarum, Villæ Northamptoniæ, by Christopher A. Markham, F.S.A.—Thomas Brittou, the Musical Small-Coal Man, by E. E. Cohen—Old Scarlett, the Peterborough Sexton—Accounts of Towcester Constables, by John Nicholson—Miserere Shoemaker of Wellingborough, by T. Tindall Wildridge—Sir Thomas Tresham and his Buildings, by John T. Page—Northamptonshire Folk-Lore, by John Nicholson—Northamptonshire Proverbs—An Ancient Hospital, by the Rev. I. Wodhams, M.A.—A carefully prepared Index—*Numerous Illustrations.*

PRESS OPINIONS.

"The volume is very interesting, and for those who dwell in the county, or whose tastes lead them to explore its history, it will have especial attraction."—*Publishers' Circular.*

"A welcome contribution to the literature of the county."—*Northampton Herald.*

"The book is published in a form that is well worthy of the high standard that the Hull Press has achieved, and we can congratulate Mr. Andrews on adding one more stone to the fabric of the bygone history of the Midlands."—*Hull Daily News.*

"An interesting volume, as well as being got up in exceptionally good style. The matter is well chosen and well rendered, so that the book is not only a thing of beauty, but also a veritable treasure-house of reliable and entertaining articles."—*Beverley Independent.*

"A welcome addition to the shelves of anyone interested in the antiquities of Northamptonshire, while even those who are not, will be able to pleasantly while away many odd half-hours by perusing its pages."—*Kettering Leader.*

HULL: WILLIAM ANDREWS & CO., THE HULL PRESS.
LONDON: HUTCHINSON & Co.

Elegantly bound in cloth gilt, demy 8vo., price 7s. 6d.

Only 750 copies printed, and each copy numbered.

Bygone Essex:

Its History, Folk-Lore, and Memorable Men and Women.

EDITED BY WILLIAM ANDREWS, F.R.H.S.,

Author of "Bygone England," "Old-Time Punishments," "Curiosities of the Church," "Old Church Lore."

CONTENTS.

Historic Essex, by Thomas Frost—Epping Forest: Its History, Customs, and Laws, by Jesse Quail—Greenstead Church, by Edward Lamplough—The Burial of Harold at Waltham, by William Winters, F.R.H.S.—St. Osyth's Priory, by John T. Page—Colchester in Olden Times, by Joseph W. Spurgeon—The Siege of Colchester, by Joseph W. Spurgeon—Colchester: Its Historic Buildings and Famous Men, by Joseph W. Spurgeon—Essex Tokens, by Thomas Forster—Queen Elizabeth at Tilbury: A Glance at Armada Days, by Edward Lamplough—The Lawless Court, by the Rev. Geo. S. Tyack, B.A.—The Dunmow Flitch—A Deserted Primitive Village, by G. Fredk. Beaumont—William Hunter: The Young Martyr of Brentwood, by John W. Odling—Fairlop Fair, by John W. Odling—Thomas Tusser, and his "Five Hundred Points of Good Husbandry," by W. H. Thompson—John Ray, Naturalist, by W. H. Thompson—Wanstead House, by John T. Page—Hopkins, the Witchfinder, by Frederick Ross, F.R.H.S.—An Essex Poet, by the Rev. Geo. S. Tyack, B.A.—Historic Harwich—Old Bow Bridge, by John T. Page—Index.

PRESS OPINIONS.

"Readable as well as instructive, and it has an interest for many more than Essex people."—*The Globe.*

"Good paper, good type, and good illustrations all help to make 'Bygone Essex' an exceedingly pleasant and agreeable book."—*Sala's Journal.*

"This work will be welcomed by all intelligent explorers of their own country, who cannot fail to regard its ancient monuments and historic localities with renewed interest after perusing it."—*The Gentlewoman.*

HULL: WILLIAM ANDREWS & CO., THE HULL PRESS.
Colchester: T. Forster.
London: Hutchinson & Co.

Elegantly bound in cloth gilt, demy 8vo., 7s. 6d.

Only 750 copies printed, and each copy numbered.

Bygone Lancashire.
Edited by ERNEST AXON.

Contents :—Historic Lancashire, by Ernest Axon—The Religious Life of Lancashire during the Commonwealth, by W. A. Shaw, M.A.—Kersal Moor, by Janet Armytage—A Lancaster Worthy (Thomas Covell), by William Hewitson—Some Early Manchester Grammar School Boys, by Ernest Axon—The Sworn Men of Amounderness, by Lieut.-Col. Henry Fishwick, F.S.A.—Lancashire Sundials, by William E. A. Axon, M.R.S.L.—The Plague in Liverpool, by J. Cooper Morley—The Old Dated Bell at Claughton, by Robert Langton, F.R.H.S.—The Children of Tim Bobbin, by Ernest Axon—The "Black Art" at Bolton—An Infant Prodigy in 1679, by Arthur W. Croxton—Wife Desertion in the Olden Times—The Colquitt Family of Liverpool—Some Old Lancashire Punishments—Bury Simnels—Eccles Wakes, by H. Cottam—Furness Abbey—Colonel Rosworm and the Siege of Manchester, by George C. Yates, F.S.A.—Poems of Lancashire Places, by William E. A. Axon, M.R.S.L.—Father Arrowsmith's Hand, by Rushworth Armytage—Index—*Illustrated.*

PRESS OPINIONS.

" A work of considerable historical and archæological interest."—*Liverpool Daily Post.*

" The book is handsomely got up."—*Manchester Guardian.*

" In the collection of papers forming this highly interesting volume, many antiquarian and historical matters connected with the County Palatine are dealt with, and at least a dozen authors have contributed essays rich in curious facts. . . All the articles are good, and should make this volume a favourite among the historical students of the County Palatine."—*Liverpool Mercury.*

" The book is excellently printed and bound."—*Library Review.*

" ' Bygone Lancashire ' is a welcome addition to the literature of the county, and we may echo the hope expressed by the editor that its appearance ' may encourage the local patriotism which is such a striking characteristic of the Lancashire Lad.' It may be added that the work, which contains a few illustrations, is well got up, and does credit to the publishers."—*Manchester Courier.*

" This is another of those clearly-printed, well-covered, readable, accurate, and entertaining ' Bygone ' volumes that come forth with pleasant frequency from the Andrews' press, Hull. . . The volume is sure of a ready sale among the more intelligent of the ' Lancashire Lads.' "—*Antiquary.*

HULL: WILLIAM ANDREWS & CO., THE HULL PRESS.
London : Hutchinson & Co.

Elegantly bound in cloth gilt, demy 8vo., price 7s. 6d.

Bygone London.
By FREDERICK ROSS, F.R.H.S.,
Author of "Yorkshire Family Romance," "Legendary Yorkshire," etc.

CONTENTS.

The Walls and Gates—Episodes in the Annals of Cheapside—Bishopsgate Street Within and Without—Aldersgate Street and St. Martin's-le-Grand—Old Broad Street—Chaucer and the Tabard—The Priory of the Holy Trinity, Aldgate—Convent of the Sisters Minoresses of the Order of St. Clare, Aldgate—The Abbey of St. Mary of Graces, or East Minster—The Barons Fitzwalter, of Baynard's Castle—Sir Nicholas Brember, Knight, Lord Mayor of London—An Olden Time Bishop of London: Robert de Braybrooke—A Brave Old London Bishop: Fulco Basset—An Old London Diarist—Index.

PRESS OPINIONS.

"Mr. Ross deals with the chief episodes in the history of London architecture, and with existing London antiquities, in a garrulous, genial spirit, which renders his book generally attractive."—*The Times.*

"Beyond all doubt a more interesting and withal informing volume than 'Bygone London' it has not been our good fortune to come across for many a long day."—*The City Press.*

PRICE ONE SHILLING.

In the Temple.

CONTENTS.

In the Temple—The Knight Templars—The Devil's Own—Christmas in the Temple—How to become a Templar—On Keeping Terms—Call Parties.

"Amusing and interesting sketches."—*Law Times.*
"Pleasant gossip about the barristers' quarter."—*Gentlewoman.*
"A very pleasant little volume."—*Globe.*
"An entertaining little book."—*Manchester Examiner.*

HULL: WILLIAM ANDREWS & CO., THE HULL PRESS.
LONDON: HUTCHINSON & CO.

Elegantly bound in cloth gilt, demy 8vo., price 7s. 6d.

Bygone Derbyshire:
Its History, Romance, Folk-Lore, Curious Customs, etc.

EDITED BY WILLIAM ANDREWS, F.R.H.S.

DERBYSHIRE is rich in historical associations of an out-of-the-way character. In the pages of "Bygone Derbyshire" are presented in a readable, and at the same time in a scholar-like style, papers, profusely illustrated, bearing on such subjects as the history of the county, ancient castles, monumental brasses, gleanings from parochial records, old church lore, family romance, traditions, curious customs, witchcraft, well-dressing, old-time sports, etc., etc.

Contents:—Historic Derbyshire, by Thomas Frost—On an Early Christian Tomb at Wirksworth, by Rev. J. Charles Cox, LL.D., F.S.A.—Curious Derbyshire Lead-Mining Customs, by William Andrews, F.R.H.S.—The Place-Name Derby, by Frederick Davis, F.S.A.—Duffield Castle, by Jno. Ward—Haddon Hall—The Romance of Haddon Hall—The Ordeal of Touch—The Monumental Brasses at Tideswell, by James L. Thornely—Bolsover Castle, by Enid A. M. Cox—The Lamp of St. Helen, by T. Tindall Wildridge—Peveril Castle, by James L. Thornely—Samuel Slater, the Father of the American Cotton Manufacture, by William E. A. Axon—The Bakewell Witches, by T. Tindall Wildridge—Mary Queen of Scots in Derbyshire—The Babington Conspiracy—Eyam and its Sad Memories, by W. G. Fretton, F.S.A.—Well-Dressing, by Rev. Geo. S. Tyack, B.A.—Old-Time Football, by Theo. Arthur—After Thirty Years: An Incident of the Civil War, by Edward Lamplough—Derbyshire and the '45, by Rev. Geo. S. Tyack, B.A.—Bess of Hardwick, by Frederick Ross, F.R.H.S.—Shadows of Romance—Index.

PRESS OPINIONS.

"'Bygone Derbyshire' is a valuable and interesting contribution to local history and archæology."—*The Times.*

"The volume is pleasant reading of a most attractive county."—*Daily Telegraph.*

"A very interesting and welcome addition to the literature of Derbyshire."—*Derbyshire Courier.*

"Mr. Andrews is to be warmly complimented on the all-round excellence of his work, which forms a valuable addition to Derbyshire literature."—*Alfreton Journal.*

"A valuable addition to any library."—*Derbyshire Times.*

HULL: WILLIAM ANDREWS & CO., THE HULL PRESS.
LONDON: HUTCHINSON & CO.

Elegantly bound in cloth gilt, demy 8vo., 7s. 6d.

BYGONE LEICESTERSHIRE.

Edited by WILLIAM ANDREWS, F.R.H.S.,

Author of " Old Church Lore," " Curiosities of the Church,"
" Old-Time Punishments," etc.

Contents:

Historic Leicestershire. By Thomas Frost.—John Wiclif and Lutterworth. By John T. Page.—The Last Days of a Dynasty: An introduction to Redmore Fight.—The Battle of Bosworth. By Edward Lamplough.—Scenes at Bosworth: The Blue Boar at Leicester.—Bradgate and Lady Jane Grey. By John T. Page.—Leicester Castle. By I. W. Dickinson, B.A.—Death of Cardinal Wolsey at Leicester Abbey. By I. W. Dickinson, B.A.—Belvoir Castle.—Robert, Earl of Leicester: A Chapter of Mediæval History.—Local Proverbs and Folk Phrases. By T. Broadbent Trowsdale.—Festival Customs in Leicestershire. By Henrietta Ellis.—Witchcraft in Leicestershire. By J. Potter Briscoe, F.R.H.S.—William Lilly, The Astrologer. By W. H. Thompson. —Gleanings from Early Leicestershire Wills. By the Rev. W. G. D. Fletcher, M.A., F.S.A.—Punishments of the Past.—Laurence Ferrers, the Murderer-Earl. By T. Broadbent Trowsdale.—The Last Gibbet. By Thomas Frost.— The Ancient Water-Mills at Loughborough. By the Rev. W. G. D. Fletcher, M.A., F.S.A.—Ashby-de-la-Zouch Castle and its Associations; Ashby-de-la-Zouch and the French Prisoners. By Canon Denton, M.A.— Miss Mary Linwood: An Artist with the Needle. By William Andrews, F.R.H.S.—Street Cries. By F. T. Mott, F.R.G.S.—Minstrelsy in Leicester. By the Rev. Geo. S. Tyack, B.A.—Index.

PRESS OPINION.

"The subjects are dealt with in a popular manner, and the utmost accuracy has been observed in setting forth the more interesting phases of local history, biography, and folk-lore of Leicestershire. The book is interspersed with some capital illustrations; the whole is nicely printed, and forms an acceptable gift to any one who takes an interest in the doings of bygone days, or in the history of this especial county."—*Hull News.*

HULL: WILLIAM ANDREWS & CO., THE HULL PRESS.
London: Hutchinson & Co.

Only 750 copies printed, and each copy numbered.

Price 7s. 6d., demy 8vo.

Bygone ∔ Kent:

Its History, Romance, Folk Lore, etc., etc.

Edited by RICHARD STEAD, B.A., F.R.H.S.

(Head Master of the Folkestone Grammar School.)

Contents:—Historic Kent, by Thomas Frost—Kentish Place-Names, by R. Stead, B.A., F.R.H.S.—St. Augustine and his Mission, by the Rev. Geo. S. Tyack, B.A.—The Ruined Chapels and Chantries of Kent, by Geo. M. Arnold, J.P., D.L., F.S.A.—A Sketch of the History of the Church or Basilica of Lyminge, by the Rev. Canon R. C. Jenkins, M.A.—Canterbury Pilgrims and their Sojourn in the City, by the Rev. W. F. Foxell, B.A.—William Lambarde, the Kentish Antiquary, by Frederick Ross, F.R.H.S.—The Revolt of the Villeins in the Days of King Richard the Second, by Edward Lamplough—Royal Eltham, by Joseph W. Spurgeon—Greenwich Fair, by Thomas Frost—The Martyred Cardinal, by Frederick Ross, F.R.H.S.—The Kentish Dialects, and Pegge and Lewis, the Old County Glossarists, by R. Stead, B.A.—The King's School, Canterbury, by the Rev. J. S. Sidebotham, M.A.—Smuggling in Kent—Huguenot Homes in Kent, by S. W. Kershaw, F.S.A.—Dover Castle, by E. Wollaston Knocker—Index.

OPINIONS OF THE PRESS.

The following are selected from a large number of favourable reviews:—

"A tasteful volume. . . . The purpose of the book, 'to give a fairly representative series of pictures of Kent and Kentish life in olden times' is, beyond doubt, amply fulfilled."—*The Antiquary.*

"Nicely printed."—*Folkestone Express.*

"The work teems with interesting details of the lives and manners of our Kentish forefathers, and should be found in every library of every Kentish man."—*Tunbridge Wells Advertiser.*

"Mr. Stead and his contributors have succeeded in producing a fascinating volume that will form pleasant reading to any one with a taste for things historical or antiquarian; while the printing and illustrations are fully equal to the high standard of previous publications from the Hull Press."—*Hull Daily News.*

HULL: WILLIAM ANDREWS & CO., THE HULL PRESS.
Canterbury: H. J. Goulden.
London: Hutchinson and Co.

Elegantly bound in cloth gilt, price 7s. 6d.

BYGONE NOTTINGHAMSHIRE:

Its History, Romance, Folk Lore, etc., etc.

BY WILLIAM STEVENSON.

CONTENTS.

The Wapentakes—The Origin of the County—The Origin of the Town—The Earliest Recorded Visitors to the County—The Suppression of the Knights Templars—Old Sanctuary Days—Notable Instances of Sanctuary—A Note on the Beverley Sanctuary—The King's Gallows of the County—The Reign of Terror in Notts—Public Executions—Old Family Feuds—Visitations of the Plague—Visitations in the Town—Visitations in the County—Nottingham Goose Fair—The Great Priory Fair at Lenton—The Pilgrimage of Grace—The Pilgrim Fathers; or, The Founders of New England—The Descendants of the Pilgrim Fathers—Archiepiscopal Palaces—The Ancient Inns and Taverns of Nottingham—Index.

PRESS OPINIONS.

"Mr. Wm. Stevenson, of several of whose previous works Nottingham and the shire have formed the bases, adds to the list an exceedingly interesting and useful book on the county, under the title of 'Bygone Nottinghamshire,' illustrated by a large number of engravings from photographs, old prints, and other sources. The writer's aim has been to incorporate much information beyond the reach of ordinary students on the past history of the county, and thereby to prove the shire is, as he believes, rich beyond comparison in ancient lore. . . . A most pleasant addition to local history."
—*Nottingham Daily Guardian.*

"We welcome Mr. Stevenson's book as a useful addition to the literature of the county."—*Newark Advertiser.*

"This recent volume of Messrs. Andrews and Company's series of 'Bygones' is a treasure to *bona-fide* students of Nottinghamshire history. The compilation of the whole book is solely the work of Mr. W. Stevenson, an ardent and original student of local history as now accepted. The book is well illustrated, the maps and plans being most valuable. . . . We have not space to do full justice to 'Bygone Nottinghamshire,' but in heartily commending it to all readers, we may say that if judged by the mean standard of quantity alone it is good value for money; but it is more than that, for besides being a popular work, it is also an original one—an exceedingly unusual combination."—*Notts and Derbyshire Notes and Queries.*

HULL: WILLIAM ANDREWS & CO., THE HULL PRESS.
London: Hutchinson & Co.

Bound in cloth gilt, demy 8vo., price 7s. 6d.

Only 500 copies printed, and each copy numbered.

THE MONUMENTAL BRASSES OF LANCASHIRE AND CHESHIRE.

With some Account of the Persons Represented.

ILLUSTRATED WITH ENGRAVINGS FROM DRAWINGS BY THE AUTHOR.

By JAMES L. THORNELY.

PRESS OPINIONS.

"Mr. Thornely's book will be eagerly sought by all lovers of monumental brasses."—*London Quarterly Review.*

"Local archæologists will give a hearty welcome to this book."—*Manchester Guardian.*

"Mr. Thornely has produced a very interesting volume, as he has not only figured nearly every monumental brass within the two counties to which he has confined his researches, but in every case he has given a description also, and in some instances the genealogical information is of a high order of value."—*The Tablet.*

"A well got-up and profusely-illustrated volume."—*Manchester Examiner and Times.*

"This book is wonderfully readable for its kind, and is evidently the result of careful and painstaking labour. The chapters are well condensed, nowhere burdened with verbiage, yet sufficiently full to serve the purpose in view. The illustrations of the various brasses are exceedingly well done, and add much value and interest to the work, which should become popular in Lancashire and Cheshire."—*Warrington Guardian.*

"'The Monumental Brasses of Lancashire and Cheshire,' with some account of the persons represented, by James L. Thornely, is a volume of great antiquarian interest to residents in the two counties. It has been a labour of love, and embodies the results, as the author remarks in his preface, of many pleasant hours during a series of pilgrimages to ancient churches and sweet communings with a stately past. The plates in the volume are reproductions of pen and ink drawings made from 'rubbings,' most of which were taken by the author, and the descriptive letterpress relates to the ancestry of many old Lancashire and Cheshire families, and is full of antiquarian and historical interest."—*Liverpool Daily Post.*

"The volume is excellently printed and finished, and its production reflects great credit on its publishers—the Hull Press."—*Hull Daily News.*

"The author's artistic drawings of the brasses he describes, as may be imagined, embrace numbers of curious outlines, from the rudest to many of elegant design. Each is accompanied by as copious a description as it seems possible to obtain, the work on the whole covering over three hundred pages of well-executed letterpress. Only five hundred copies have been printed, and these have been nearly all taken up by subscribers."—*Chester Courant.*

"Messrs. William Andrews & Co., of Hull" ("Logroller" writes in the *Star*), "seem to be producing some handsome antiquarian books. The latest that has come to me is an account of 'The Monumental Brasses of Lancashire and Cheshire,' by Mr. James L. Thornely. Brass-rubbing is a most fascinating enthusiasm. 'Wouldst thou know the beauty of holiness?' asks Lamb. 'Go alone on some week-day, borrowing the keys of good Master Sexton, traverse the cool aisles of some country church.' Those cool aisles are the workshop of the brass-rubber. While he kneels over his spread sheet of paper, and diligently plies his 'heel-ball,' the afternoon lights dapple the old stones, and country sounds and scents steal in to keep him company at his solitary task. You see I also have been in Arcady. Mr. Thornely is not only interested in his subject himself, but he has the gift of imparting his interest to others. His accounts of his various brasses and the personages they commemorate are simple and clear, and marked by a literary touch too rare in the treatment of such themes."

HULL: WILLIAM ANDREWS & CO., THE HULL PRESS.
LONDON: HUTCHINSON & CO.

b

Elegantly bound in cloth gilt, demy 8vo., 6s.

⋊ Legendary ∗ Yorkshire. ⋉
By FREDERICK ROSS, F.R.H.S.

Contents: The Enchanted Cave—The Doomed City—The Worm of Nunnington—The Devil's Arrows—The Giant Road Maker of Mulgrave—The Virgin's Head of Halifax—The Dead Arm of St. Oswald the King—The Translation of St. Hilda—A Miracle of St. John—The Beatified Sisters—The Dragon of Wantley—The Miracles and Ghost of Watton—The Murdered Hermit of Eskdale—The Calverley Ghost—The Bewitched House of Wakefield.

PRESS OPINIONS.

Beverley Recorder says—"It is a work of lasting interest, and cannot fail to delight the reader."

Driffield Observer says—"The history and the literature of our county are now receiving marked attention, and Mr. Andrews merits the support of the public for the production of this and the other interesting volumes he has issued. We cannot speak too highly of this volume, the printing, the paper, and the binding being faultless."

Elegantly bound in cloth gilt, demy 8vo., 6s.

Yorkshire Family Romance.
By FREDERICK ROSS, F.R.H.S.

Contents:—The Synod of Streoneshalh—The Doomed Heir of Osmotherley—St. Eadwine, the Royal Martyr—The Viceroy Siward—Phases in the Life of a Political Martyr—The Murderer's Bride—The Earldom of Wiltes—Black-faced Clifford—The Shepherd Lord—The Felons of Ilkley—The Ingilby Boar's Head—The Eland Tragedy—The Plumpton Marriage—The Topcliffe Insurrection—Burning of Cottingham Castle—The Alum Workers—The Maiden of Marblehead—Rise of the House of Phipps—The Traitor Governor of Hull.

PRESS OPINIONS.

"The grasp and thoroughness of the writer is evident in every page, and the book forms a valuable addition to the literature of the North Country."—*Gentlewoman.*

"Many will welcome this work."—*Yorkshire Post.*

HULL: WILLIAM ANDREWS & CO., THE HULL PRESS.
LONDON: HUTCHINSON & CO.

Paper Cover, 1s. Cloth, 2s.

My Christ: and other Poems.
By H. ELVET LEWIS.
(ELFED.)

"The fifty pages, by no means overcrowded, which Mr. Elvet Lewis has given us, go far to justify the hope that a new poet of genuine power has arisen among us. The thought is often singularly beautiful. The expression is so simple and so natural that it conceals the art. The delicacy of the workmanship may easily blind us to the strength. Mr. Lewis is essentially original, though his affinities are closest, perhaps, to Whittier and Lynch : but there is not a trace of imitation to be found in the book from one end to the other."—*Literary World.*

"This little volume possesses a rare charm for the lovers of really good verse. The writer is evidently of the number of those whose spirituality is intense, and whose faith in, and hold of, the things "not seen and eternal" are vivid and strong. The opening poem, which gives the work its title—'My Christ' is singularly beautiful for the spirit of love, loyalty, and devotion which it breathes in every line. Altogether, the poems are of a high order, and quite worthy of ranking alongside such works as 'The Lyra Innocentium' and 'The Christian Year.'"—*Hull Times.*

"The verses are worthy of Mr. Lewis' poetic genius, and breathe a spirit of devotion which will certainly have an uplifting influence upon those who peruse the verses. Mr. Lewis has a pure style, and in the poems before us there are a few gems of thought which shew their originator to be an author of great ability."—*Llanelly Guardian.*

"Sacred poems of great merit and beauty."—*Newcastle Daily Chronicle.*

Fancy Cover, 1s.

Wanted--An Heiress : A Novel.
By EVAN MAY.

"It is an entrancing story, and perfectly wholesome reading. In this work, the author of 'The Greatest of These' is at her best ; and 'Wanted, an Heiress' may be pronounced a leading tale of the season."—*South Yorkshire Free Press.*

"The story is well told."—*Northern Echo.*

"It is a bright book for holiday reading.—*Carlisle Express.*

HULL: WILLIAM ANDREWS & CO., THE HULL PRESS.
LONDON : HUTCHINSON & CO.

Price 6s.   Demy 8vo.   Elegantly bound in cloth gilt.

A Month in a Dandi:

A Woman's Wanderings in Northern India.

By CHRISTINA S. BREMNER.

Contents.—The Ascent from the Plains to the Hills—Kasauli and its Amusements—Theories on Heat—Simla, the Queen of the Hill Stations—Starting Alone for the Interior—In Bussahir State—The Religious Festival at Pangay—On Congress—On the Growing Poverty of India.

PRESS OPINIONS.

"The author of a 'Month in a Dandi' has a facile pen, and is evidently a shrewd observer. Her book differs from many belonging to the same class by reason of its freshness, its spontaneity, and its abundance of interesting detail. Moreover, the book is written with a purpose. 'If by perusing these pages the reader obtains a clearer view of England's attitude to her great dependency, if his prepossessions against 'black men' and the 'poor heathen' should melt away in any degree, if the assumption that what is good for England must necessarily be so for India receives a slight shake, the writer will feel rewarded.' To these conclusions one is almost certain to come when the experiences of Miss Bremner's 'Month in a Dandi' are recalled. There would be no end to our quotations were we to reproduce all the passages we have marked as being interesting. Miss Bremner is always in good spirits, and writes with ease, and evidently *con amore.*"—*Birmingham Daily Gazette.*

"Miss Bremner's book describes a woman's wanderings in Northern India, and it is written from adequate knowledge, with shrewd discernment, and a pleasing amount of vivacity.—*Speaker.*

"'A Month in a Dandi' is full of instruction It shows a great deal of ability and determination to express truths, even if they be unpalatable. The chapters on the vexed questions of Baboo culture and Indian Congress are well worth reading."—*Manchester Guardian.*

"Miss Bremner's style is chastened for the most part, humorous, faithful to detail, and oftentimes polished to literary excellence. The earlier chapters are full of raciness and agreeable personality."—*Hull Daily Mail.*

"'A Month in a Dandi' describes the writer's wanderings in Northern India, following upon a shrewdly observant account of the seamy side of Anglo-Indian Society. The subject throughout is approached from a political economist's point of view. The chapter on the growing poverty of India sounds a warning note."—*Gentlewoman.*

"The author of a 'Month in a Dandi' is evidently a keen observer of men and things, and we know that her opinion is shared by many of our countrymen who have had a much larger experience of India and Indian affairs than herself. The book is full of the most exquisite word pictures, pictures that are full of light, beauty, and grace, but, unfortunately, some of them have more shade than we care to see; but, doubtless, Miss Bremner's treatment is correct and life-like."—*Hull Daily News.*

HULL: WILLIAM ANDREWS & CO., THE HULL PRESS.
London: Hutchinson & Co.

"Quite up to Date."—Hull Daily Mail.

Crown 8vo., 140 pp.; fancy cover, 1s.; cloth bound, 2s.

STEPPING-STONES TO SOCIALISM.
BY DAVID MAXWELL, C E.

CONTENTS

In a reasonable and able manner Mr. Maxwell deals with the following topics:—The Popular Meaning of the Term Socialism—Lord Salisbury on Socialism—Why There is in Many Minds an Antipathy to Socialism—On Some Socialistic Views of Marriage—The Question of Private Property—The Old Political Economy is not the Way of Salvation—Who is My Neighbour?—Progress, and the Condition of the Labourer—Good and Bad Trade: Precarious Employment—All Popular Movements are Helping on Socialism—Modern Literature in Relation to Social Progress—Pruning the Old Theological Tree—The Churches,—Their Socialistic Tendencies—The Future of the Earth in Relation to Human Life—Socialism is Based on Natural Laws of Life—Humanity in the Future—Preludes to Socialism—Forecasts of the Ultimate Form of Society—A Pisgah-top View of the Promised Land.

PRESS OPINIONS.

The following are selected from a large number of favourable notices:—

" The author has evidently reflected deeply on the subject of Socialism, and his views are broad, equitable, and quite up to date. In a score or so of chapters he discusses Socialism from manifold points of view, and in its manifold aspects. Mr. Maxwell is not a fanatic; his book is not dull, and his style is not amateurish."—*Hull Daily Mail.*

"There is a good deal of charm about Mr. Maxwell's style."—*Northern Daily News.*

" The book is well worthy of perusal."—*Hull News.*

" The reader who desires more intimate acquaintance with a subject that is often under discussion at the present day, will derive much interest from a perusal of this little work. Whether it exactly expresses the views of the various socialists themselves is another matter, but inasmuch as these can seldom agree even among themselves, the objection is scarcely so serious as might otherwise be thought."—*Publishers' Circular.*

HULL: WILLIAM ANDREWS & CO., THE HULL PRESS.
London: Hutchinson & Co.

Elegantly bound in cloth gilt, crown 8vo., 340 pp., 4/4 nett.

ANDREWS' LIBRARY OF POPULAR FICTION.

No. 1.—Children of Chance.
By HERBERT LLOYD.

PRESS OPINIONS.

"Mr. Lloyd has redeemed his story by sprightly incident and some admirable character sketches. Madge, whom the hero eventually marries, is a charming creation, and yet 'not too light and good for human nature's daily food.' Her sister and her husband, Tom Coltman, are also a fine couple, and Mr. Lloyd introduces us to some very clever scenes at the theatre at which they perform. The hero's sister, Gladys, is another favourite, and the family to which she is introduced consists of many persons in whom the reader is bound to take an interest. Mr. Lloyd works up the climax in a truly masterly manner, and the discovery of the father of the 'children of chance,' is ingenious and clever. In short we have little but praise for this book. . . . The reader's interest is aroused from the first and is sustained to the end. There is pathos in the story and there is humour, and Mr. Lloyd writes very gracefully and tenderly where grace and tenderness are needed."—*Birmingham Daily Gazette.*

"The story . . . is full of action and movement, and is never dull."—*The Scotsman.*

"Messrs. William Andrews & Co., of Hull, have opened their 'Library of Popular Fiction' with a brightly-written novel by Herbert Lloyd, entitled 'Children of Chance.' The treatment of the story is distinctly above the average. . . . The character of Richard Framley, though a minor one, is very cleverly limned, and a forcible piece of writing in the last chapter but one, will leave a vivid impression even to the reader who merely skims the book. Altogether the 'Library' has reached a high standard with its initial volume."—*Eastbourne Observer.*

"Those who can appreciate a good story told in plain and simple language will probably find a good deal of pleasure in perusing 'Children of Chance,' by Herbert Lloyd. It is altogether devoid of sensationalism. At the same time one feels an interest in the various couples who are introduced, and whose love-making is recorded in a very agreeable manner. . . . Mr. Lloyd succeeds in depicting an effective scene at the final *denouement*, the period before it being attractively filled in. It is artistically worked out."—*Sala's Journal.*

"The story is strengthened by the interest attaching to its women, and by a certain lightness of touch and naturalness in the portrayal of the life of an artistic family. Some of the characters are both well drawn and likeable, and one or two strong incidents redeem the general tone of the plot."—*Glasgow Herald.*

"This is decidedly a good novel, and the plot is sufficiently exciting to attract a reader and hold him to the end."—*The Publishers' Circular.*

"The author of 'Children of Chance,' grasps one of the first essentials of fiction, dramatic effect. . . . There is no lack of new ideas, and the story is not uninteresting."—*The Literary World.*

"The plot of 'Children of Chance,' by Herbert Lloyd, is in many ways a powerful one. . . . There are several strong situations, and the book is well worth reading."—*The Yorkshire Post.*

"'Children of Chance,' which inaugurates Andrews' 'Library of Popular Fiction,' enforces the lesson of evil consequences that may be expected to follow upon foul deeds deliberately wrought. . . . The interest in the career of Cecil Studholme and his children is kept well alive."—*The Academy.*

"This is a well-balanced and cleverly written novel. Some fine realistic work is displayed in the delineation of several characters, a trait which shows that the author has kept a high ideal before him in his constructive processes. . . . Love episodes come in, and the conversation is exceedingly healthy and natural. The volume is beautifully got-up."—*The Perthshire Advertiser.*

"There is plenty of love-making in the story, several of the characters are well drawn, and the plot is an ingenious one."—*Northern Evening Mail.*

"Much of Mr. Lloyd's book is bright, fresh, and ingenious. . . . The plot is cleverly conceived, and shows careful treatment from beginning to end. . . . There are in 'Children of Chance' notable instances where a deep insight into human nature is perceptible; many scenes, such as that which closes on the life of the deserted wife, show a touch of pathos of which many a more noted author might feel justly proud; while at times the dialogue is far from indifferent.—*Hull News.*

"'Children of Chance' is the pioneer volume of Andrews' 'Library of Fiction.' It ought to win its way to popular favour. Its attractive binding and excellent printing are commendable features, while the story itself displays high literary merit. Mr. Lloyd does not lack the modern fiction writer's capacity for the creation of sensational incidents; but he manages his plots with ingenuity and success, and his morality is thoroughly sound."—*North Eastern Daily Gazette.*

HULL: WILLIAM ANDREWS & CO., THE HULL PRESS.
LONDON: HUTCHINSON & CO.

www.ingramcontent.com/pod-product-compliance
Lightning Source LLC
Chambersburg PA
CBHW030325240426
43673CB00040B/1277